Spiritual Wellness

A Personal Study
of Colossians

Spiritual Wellness

A Personal Study
of Colossians

"A Woman's Guide" Series — Revised Edition

Rhonda Harrington Kelley

NEW HOPE
PUBLISHERS

Birmingham, Alabama

New Hope Publishers
P. O. Box 12065
Birmingham, AL 35202–2065
www.newhopepublishers.com
New Hope® Publishers is a division of WMU®.

Library of Congress Cataloging-in-Publication Data

Kelley, Rhonda.
  [Woman's guide to spiritual wellness]
  Spiritual wellness : a personal study of Colossians : a woman's guide
/ Rhonda Harrington Kelley.
     p. cm.
  Originally published: A woman's guide to spiritual wellness. 1998.
  Includes bibliographical references.
  ISBN 978-1-59669-259-6 (sc)
  1. Bible. N.T. Colossians--Textbooks. 2. Christian women--Religious
life. I. Title.
  BS2715.55.K45 2010
  227'.7007--dc22
                          2010006952

ISBN-10: 1-59669-259-6
ISBN-13: 978-1-59669-259-6

N104130 • 0610 • 2M1

~ TABLE OF CONTENTS ~

~ FOREWORD ~

On a daily basis, I work diligently to take care of my physical condition. I discipline myself to exercise regularly, and I try to eat a nutritious diet. I take vitamins and see my doctor annually for a complete physical examination. And I even attempt to get proper rest. I have been taught to take care of my body, to prevent physical illness. Wellness is important to my personal life and to my ministry.

It is important for me as a Christian to be just as conscientious about spiritual wellness as I am about my physical condition. Rather than waiting for spiritual illness to occur, I work faithfully on my personal spiritual growth. Prayer, Bible study, service, and witnessing are essential prescriptions for my spiritual wellness. When I falter in building my relationship with the Lord, my spiritual condition weakens and I become susceptible to sin. The Book of Colossians has become a prescriptive medication for my own spiritual wellness. Paul's insights into Christian living have strengthened my spiritual stamina and helped me resist illness.

Walk with me through this study of the Book of Colossians and discover the care of the Great Physician!

—Rhonda Harrington Kelley

~ INTRODUCTION ~

This Bible study contains 12 lessons that thoroughly examine God's guidelines for spiritual wellness from the Book of Colossians. Several tools are necessary before you begin your personal study. First, you must make a genuine commitment to complete the study you begin. You may desire to spend time in God's Word, but you must discipline yourself to do it. Try to read through the Book of Colossians several times during your study.

Next, you should select a Bible translation that is readable and has features you prefer. (This Bible study uses the Holman Christian Standard Bible unless otherwise noted.) You may also find it helpful to read certain passages in several translations to gain additional insights. And don't hesitate to underline or write in your Bible as you begin your personal study.

Each lesson is designed to focus on one passage of Scripture, though the approach to each study varies. Some lessons are verse-by-verse studies, while others deal with the theme of the overall passage. However, each lesson encourages personal response and includes a Scripture focus (Prescription for Spiritual Wellness) and practical application (Personal Spiritual Wellness). The selected key Scripture is excellent for Bible memory. Store up these biblical truths and apply them in your daily life.

This Bible study was written for individual study. Read the Scripture and complete the study questions personally. Begin your Bible study time with prayer. Ask God to speak to you clearly, reveal Himself plainly, and increase your knowledge of His Word continually. After you pray, read the focal passage of Scripture. Reading aloud is often helpful. Take time to hear the Word, as well as see it. Answer the questions as they are asked. Each lesson should take you from 30 to 45 minutes to complete. The study is designed to last 12 weeks, with one lesson per week. Don't hurry through the study; instead, let each biblical truth become real to you.

You may also share this study of the Book of Colossians with a small group. Each person should complete their own study and then discuss it with the group. A group leader should facilitate the discussion and organize the group. One-hour sessions are suggested. Interaction with others about the Book of Colossians will enhance your learning experience and promote your spiritual growth. In addition, group participation will hold you accountable. (See the Group Teaching Guide at the back of the book for suggestions about leading a small group Bible study.)

When you have completed your study of Colossians, share what you have learned with someone else and apply what God has taught you in your daily life. Bible study should make a difference in your life and in the lives of others. You will be strengthened spiritually, and you will promote spiritual wellness in your own life. May God richly bless your Bible study!

Lesson 1
Called by Christ
Introduction

Physicians today are focusing medical interventions more on prevention than on treatment. Most prefer physical wellness for the body over the treatment of illness. Believers should challenge themselves to seek spiritual wellness for the soul. Wellness involves the total person. Therefore, individuals should care for themselves physically, spiritually, emotionally, and mentally. Women are particularly challenged to juggle the many demands of their busy lives so they can nurture their families and manage their responsibilities.

The Book of Colossians contains many theological truths and doctrinal statements, but it can also be used as a practical guide for women moving toward a lifestyle of spiritual wellness. Paul, himself, gave instruction and encouragement to his Christian friends in Colossae who were facing spiritual challenges. His inspired words from God became a prescription for spiritual wellness and can guide Christians today. This study is designed to help you better understand the biblical teachings of Colossians and apply those godly principles in your lives today.

My prayer is for you to become healthier as you dig into the Word of God and for you to develop a lifestyle of wellness that will strengthen and sustain you for the rest of your life. As we begin our journey toward spiritual wellness, let's investigate the background of the Book of Colossians.

The Author

The New Testament letter of Colossians [kuh-LAHSH-uhnz] was undoubtedly written by the apostle Paul (Colossians 1:1). Timothy, his friend in faith, was with Paul and probably served as his stenographer, actually penning the letter. And, Tychicus [TIK-ih-kuhs] probably served as courier of the letter to the Christians in Colossae. Though Paul apparently had not visited the city or founded the church there, he had personal interest in the Christians at Colossae (Colossians 2:1).

Read Colossians 1:1 and 2:1. Who wrote the Book of Colossians?

_____

Who was with him?

_____

_____

Had Paul visited Colossae?

_____

What phrase supports your answer?

_____

_____

_____

In recent history, some biblical scholars have questioned the authorship of this letter primarily for three reasons:

1. Some say that the Book of Colossians contains words and phrases not typical of Paul's other writings.

2. Some say that gnostic thought, which is a prominent subject in the Book of Colossians, did not develop until a much later time than that of Paul.

3. The view of Christ recorded in Colossians is more advanced than any other of Paul's discussions of Christ.

Most scholars today accept Paul's authorship of Colossians. He identified himself as author in verse one; he expressed himself in different ways by the inspiration of God; he definitely encountered the roots of gnostic thinking; and over time and through new experiences, he developed his understanding of Christ.

What do you know about the man Paul?

_____

_____

_____

_____

_____

Paul was a Jew who experienced a dramatic conversion. He was a faithful Christian who started many churches and wrote 13 books of the New Testament.

His Birth

Saul was born in Tarsus (Acts 22:3), a bustling city in southern Turkey, in approximately A.D. 1–5. Scripture records that he was born a Jew, raised strictly as a Jew, and served faithfully as a Jewish leader. In fact, Saul became known as *"a Hebrew born of Hebrews"* (Philippians 3:5) because of his adherence to Old Testament laws and traditions and his scholarly training to teach the Scriptures. Paul documented his credentials in the third chapter of Philippians. He was *"circumcised the eighth day"* according to Jewish tradition. He was *"of the nation of Israel"* since his Jewish heritage traced back to Jacob and Rachel. He was *"of the tribe of Benjamin,"* the tribe that produced Israel's first king, Saul, for whom he may have been named. He was a *"Hebrew born of Hebrews"* since both his parents were Jews and he was raised as a strict Jew. He was *"a Pharisee,"* a member of the legalistic Jewish sect and the son of a Pharisee. He was also a persecutor of the church. Scripture says that he *"was ravaging the church, and he would enter house after house, and drag off men and women, and put them in prison"* (Acts 8:3).

How does Paul describe himself in Colossians 1:1 and 1:23?

_____

_____

_____

He describes himself as *"an apostle of Christ Jesus"* and *"a minister."*

How does his preconversion identity compare with his postconversion identity? (Compare Philippians 3:3–6 and Colossians 1:1,23.)

_____

_____

_____

_____

_____

_____

_____

_____

Before Christ, Paul was a circumcised Jew, a legalistic Pharisee, persecutor of the church, and an obedient law follower (Philippians 3:3–6). After his conversion, he was an apostle of Christ and a minister of the gospel (Colossians 1:1, 23).

Scripture provides much biographical information about Paul, his life before Christ and his life after Christ. His conversion experience is one of the most dramatic recorded testimonies.

His Rebirth

Acts 9:1–19 records the conversion and baptism of Saul of Tarsus. **Read this passage; then briefly summarize the salvation testimony of Saul.**

_____

_____

_____

_____

_____

_____

Saul of Tarsus, who boasted of his persecution of the Christians, later experienced a dramatic conversion to faith in Jesus Christ. Paul was traveling to Damascus in approximately A.D. 34–35 to arrest Jewish people who had accepted Jesus as Messiah. Suddenly, Saul saw a bright light and heard God speak. Blind and helpless but obedient, he was led into Damascus to a disciple named Ananias, who told Saul he had been chosen as God's messenger to the Gentiles. By faith, Saul was saved, filled with the Holy Spirit, and called to ministry. He received his sight and was baptized.

His Life

After his conversion, Saul grew in his faith and began to preach Christ, first to his own people, the Jews, and then to the Gentiles. Though his parents had given him the name Saul, after his conversion he became known by the name Paul, his official Roman name (Acts 13:9). As he traveled, Paul preached the gospel, started churches, and made disciples. His strong stand for Christ caused him to become the *persecuted*, not the *persecutor*.

Paul's life is characterized by many significant events including:

- First trip to Jerusalem in A.D. 37–38 (Acts 9:26–29)

- Second trip to Jerusalem in A.D. 48 (Acts 11:27–30)

- Philippi imprisonment in A.D. 58–60 (Acts 16:16–40)

- Caesarean imprisonment in A.D. 58–60 (Acts 23:23–26:32)

- Roman imprisonment in A.D. 60–63 (Acts 27–28)

Choose one of the above accounts in the life of Paul to read. After reading the passage carefully, write a short summary of the event.

_____

_____

_____

_____

_____

_____

Paul's first visit to Jerusalem was memorable. He was shunned by many followers of Christ but befriended by Barnabas. His preaching ministry began as did his persecution by Hellenistic Jews (Acts 9:26–29). Paul escaped to Caesarea then Tarsus but later returned to Jerusalem along with other prophets. Paul and Barnabas delivered financial support to the leaders of the churches (Acts 11:27–30).

Paul's ministry continued and his persecution by the Jews escalated. In about A.D. 58–60, Paul and his co-laborer Silas were imprisoned in Philippi on charges of disturbing the city with their preaching and miracles. They were beaten and jailed, but they still praised the Lord by singing. An earthquake shook the jail and startled the jailer. But, Paul and Silas did not escape. Instead they led the jailer and his family to Christ (Acts 16:16–40).

Again, Paul was imprisoned in Caesarea, accused before the governor Felix of leading a rebel sect and desecrating the temple. He defended himself and then appealed to Caesar and later to King Agrippa with opportunities to share his testimony. In the end, Paul was released and sent to Rome (Acts 23:23–26:32).

After a tumultuous voyage, Paul was again imprisoned for speaking the gospel. His ministry in Rome was confined by his house arrest. He preached about the kingdom of God, using Old Testament Scriptures to persuade the Jews that Jesus was the Messiah. His two-year imprisonment in Rome was a productive time during which he wrote the Prison Epistles—Ephesians, Colossians, Philemon, and Philippians during that imprisonment.

His Journeys

During his ministry, the Apostle Paul, along with other followers of Christ, embarked on missions trips to spread the gospel to unsaved people. Among his traveling companions were Barnabas, John Mark, Luke, Silas, and Timothy. The Holy Spirit blessed their endeavors as many people were saved and many churches were started. These four trips have become known as Paul's Missionary Journeys.

1. First missionary journey in A.D. 48–50 to Galatia and Cyprus (Acts 13–14);

2. Second missionary journey in A.D. 51–53 to Macedonia, Achaia, and Greece (Acts 15:39–18:22);

3. Third missionary journey in A.D. 54–57 to Asia and Greece (Acts 18:23–21:17); and

4. Fourth missionary journey as he traveled to prison in Rome in A.D. 59–60 to Caesarea, Crete, Malta, and Rome (Acts 27–28).

If your Bible has a section of maps, find the Mediterranean Sea and trace the four missionary journeys of Paul the apostle. More than any other disciple, Paul touched the world of his day with the gospel.

His Writings

Paul the apostle is certainly well known for his dramatic conversion, his faithful life, and his missionary journeys. But he is best known for his prolific biblical writing. This one man wrote 13 books of the New Testament, letters to the Christians of his world. His epistles comprise one-fifth of the entire Bible and contain many significant theological truths.

The Book of Colossians was Paul's ninth letter, written in A.D. 60–63. Though there is some uncertainty about the precise dating of the Pauline Epistles, most modern theologians accept the following chronology.

1. 1 Thessalonians — A.D. 50–52

2. 2 Thessalonians — A.D. 51–52

3. Galatians — A.D. 55–57

4. 1 Corinthians — A.D. 56–57

5. 2 Corinthians — A.D. 56–57

6. Romans — A.D. 55–59

7. Ephesians — A.D. 60–63

8. Philippians — A.D. 60–63

9. Colossians — A.D. 60–63

10. Philemon — A.D. 60–63

11. 1 Timothy — A.D. 62–64

12. Titus — A.D. 62–64

13. 2 Timothy — A.D. 66–67

Which of these letters written by Paul has strengthened you most spiritually?

_____

_____

_____

Why?

_____

_____

_____

_____

_____

Letters of ancient times had a particular literary form that you see clearly in the Book of Colossians. This epistle includes these components:

Salutation — References are made to the sender and to the recipient of the letter together with a greeting.

Thanksgiving and/or Prayer — All of Paul's letters, except Galatians where its absence is significant, include this element.

Body — This section is typically the longest part of Paul's letters.

Exhortation — These specific instructions are directed to the congregation, depending upon their respective situations and needs.

Conclusion — Words calling for peace, greetings to friends, and/or closing blessings are included.

His Death

According to Acts 28:30–31, Paul "stayed two whole years in his own rented house. And he welcomed all who visited him, proclaiming the kingdom of God and teaching the things concerning the Lord Jesus Christ with full boldness and without hindrance."

Few specific details are known about Paul's death. Scholars believe that he was released from prison in Rome and ministered in the west, probably Spain. Later he returned to Rome and was imprisoned for a second time, during which he wrote the Pastoral Epistles — 1 and 2 Timothy and Titus. Paul was martyred for his faith. It is said that he was beheaded outside the city gates of Rome in A.D. 65 when Nero was persecuting Christians. Because he gave his life for the spreading of the gospel, Paul will always be one of the greatest martyrs of the faith.

His Audience

Each of Paul's letters was written to a specific New Testament church congregation or individual, but all of his letters are also addressed to Christians today. In Colossians, Paul addresses the saints (in Greek *hagiois*) or those "set apart," the faithful followers of Christ. While he did not always know his audience personally, he was aware of their circumstances and concerned about their challenges. This letter, written while Paul was imprisoned in Rome, was to be read aloud to a congregation as encouragement and warning. It was written specifically to the people of the church at Colossae. Though a Jewish community existed around Colossae, the church was probably composed mainly of Gentile believers (Colossians 1:27). Let us examine the city, the church, and the conflict.

The City

Located in the southwest corner of Asia Minor, or present day Turkey, Colossae [koh-LAHS-sih] was a prominent city during the Greek period. Located at the base of Mount Cadmus (elevation 8,435 feet), Colossae was about 120 miles east of Ephesus in the Lycus River Valley. It was a major trade route and was home to a significant Jewish population. However, by the time of Paul, this city had become overshadowed by many neighboring towns, such as Laodicea [lay-AHD-ih-SEE-uh]. Its greatest resource was its fertile land where sheep were raised for the wool industry.

Colossae became famous for a certain dye for clothing that bears its name. Though its geographical location seemed ideal, Colossae and the area around it experienced frequent earthquakes. In fact, the city was destroyed in A.D. 61 by a severe earthquake.

Search your New Testament map and locate the town of Colossae in southwest Asia Minor.

Nothing exists of Colossae today. The mounds of dirt thought to be the ancient city have yet to be excavated by archeologists.

Certainly, much history of the once significant city could be validated if the ruins were uncovered.

The Church

The church at Colossae consisted predominantly of Gentile believers with a small number of Jewish converts. Though Paul did not visit this area himself, the church was probably started during his evangelization of Ephesus. Epaphras [EP-uh-frass] is described as the faithful minister of the Colossian church (Colossians 1:7; 4:12–13). He was also called a fellow servant of Paul. He told Paul of the spiritual state of the church, especially of the influence of heretical teachings.

Read these verses and describe the Christians in Colossae— Colossians 1:2, 12, 21, 27.

_____

_____

_____

_____

_____

_____

Paul described the Colossian Christians as saints, faithful, qualified to partake in the inheritance, once alienated now reconciled, and the recipients of God's mystery.

The Conflict

New Christians in the Colossian church were being challenged by false teaching or heresy. Heresy refers to any teaching that is rejected by the Christian community because it is contrary to

Scripture. While numerous distorted viewpoints prevailed, the roots of gnostic thought were evident in Colossae at the time of Paul's letter. The *Women's Evangelical Commentary: New Testament* says gnosticism was "an early Greek religious movement whose followers believed that they gained special kind of spiritual knowledge that was unavailable to most people." The root of the word *gnosticism* is the Greek word *gnosis* meaning "knowledge."

Gnosticism has two basic assumptions: (1) the spirit alone is good and matter is evil; and (2) the universe is created out of matter that is both evil and eternal. Those teachings greatly affected the doctrine of creation, the gift of salvation, and the ethical approach to life. Thus, a conflict arose between the Christians in Colossae and the false teachers.

Read Colossians 2:8–10 and write a warning to all Christians who encounter heresies.

_____

_____

_____

_____

_____

All Christians are warned to beware of heresy and false teaching that will deceive them, and to follow only Christ.

His Admonition

Paul wrote his letters for the same reason people write letters and postcards today—to keep in touch with family and friends. Paul particularly wanted to stay in touch with those he cared about while traveling. This letter was written to his friends in

Colossae. In fact, Paul desired for this letter to be read aloud to a congregation.

What impact does reading a letter aloud have on the listener?

_____

_____

_____

_____

_____

Reading a letter aloud holds attention, gives expression to the text, and becomes memorable. Paul obviously wanted his message to be heard. He had a strong admonition for the Colossian Christians. His warning in Colossians 1:27–28 states his purpose: the gospel of Jesus Christ is for all people. Therefore, we are called by Christ to proclaim His truth to everyone—the Jews and Gentiles, people we know, and even strangers. That same message speaks to Christians today. We are to go into the whole world and share the good news of Jesus Christ with every man and woman regardless of race, ethnicity, gender, class, education, or background.

His Answers

In his short but powerful letter, Paul attempts to answer some difficult questions with practical theological insights. His purposes were to combat false teachings and instruct Christians in truth. As a result, he develops several themes. These profound answers are practical guidelines for daily living. As you read the Book of Colossians, notice these primary themes:

1. Christ is Creator of everything and Savior of all.

2. The world is sinful and seeking to devour all.

3. Christians are vehicles of service and examples of faith. These major themes are foundational to a Christian's life and to the work of the church.

Paul used two words to describe the Christian life to the Colossians—*freedom* and *fullness*. Freedom is available to all believers through Jesus Christ who died on the cross to provide salvation (Colossians 2:14). And, fullness of life is offered to all who live out their faith daily.

Prescription 1 for Spiritual Wellness

"Grace to you and peace from God our Father" (Colossians 1:2).

Personal Spiritual Wellness

Who are you? In many ways, your identity is wrapped up in your relationship with Christ. Read these two passages of Scripture: Colossians 1:21–22 and Colossians 2:10.

How does Paul describe you?

_____

_____

_____

_____

_____

Now read 1 Peter 2:9–10.

List some words or phrases that identify who you are in Christ.

_____

_____

_____

_____

_____

Thank God for who you are and who He intends for you to be!

Lesson 2
Prayer Pleases God
Colossians 1:1–12

Introduction

Most Christians receive great joy as they talk to the Father. But have you ever thought that prayer pleases God? The Lord wants to hear from His children. Though He already knows our thoughts and desires, God loves for us to voice our hearts to Him.

One prescription for spiritual wellness is prayer. Believers cannot grow in their faith without communicating with God. Prayer is an essential ingredient for spiritual growth. Jesus Himself commanded us to pray, but He didn't ask us to pray without teaching us how.

In the Book of Colossians, we learn to pray by Paul's example and instruction. Initially, Paul greeted the Christians in Colossae. Then he gave three specific ways to pray: lift up others, thank the Father, and ask for power. Carefully read Colossians 1:1–12 and underline any instructions about prayer.

Lift Up Others

Christians are greatly encouraged by the prayers of others. It is both a privilege and a responsibility to talk with God about the concerns of other people. Paul reminds us of his own prayers for fellow Christians and challenges us to lift up each other in prayer.

What specific prayer did Paul voice for the Colossians in verse 2?

He prayed: "_____ to you and _____ from God our Father."

Paul often introduced his letters to the churches with a greeting and a prayer. He typically extended *grace* and *peace* to his readers. **Why is it important to pray for grace and peace for others?**

_____

_____

_____

_____

_____

_____

The most powerful prayer a Christian can pray for another Christian is for grace and peace. Grace is the unmerited gift of God that provides for our salvation. Peace is the sense of well-being regardless of outward circumstances. A believer needs grace for salvation and peace for Christian living. Both are acknowledged to be *"from God our Father"* (v. 2).

Paul gave additional instruction in Colossians 1:1–12 on how to lift up others in prayer.

Read each of these verses from Colossians and write one guideline about praying for another person.

1:3 _____

1:9 _____

1:10 _____

1:11 _____

1:12 _____

Encouragement of others is a common teaching of the New Testament. Everyone needs to be lifted up, and everyone needs to lift up others. Prayer is a specific way to encourage and be encouraged. As we pray for others, offer thanks for them (v. 3). Ask God to fill them with knowledge, wisdom, and spiritual understanding (v. 9). Pray specifically that they will walk worthy of the Lord, please Him, bear fruit, and grow spiritually (v. 10). Seek strength, endurance, and patience for them from the Lord (v. 11). And, give thanks to God that you are able to serve Him together (v. 12).

While the Lord is eager to hear about our own needs, He is pleased when we talk with Him about others. Our friends need our prayers. We need to pray for others. And, God is glorified as we pray.

Look up the definition of the words *supplication, petition,* **and** *intercession* **in the dictionary. Compare these prayer words in the space provided.**

_____

_____

_____

_____

_____

_____

Supplication generally refers to the humble, earnest act of requesting. While petition is the request a believer makes for her own needs, intercession is prayer focused on the needs of others. Your prayertime should always be humble and earnest including praise to your Father and intercession for others as well as petitions for yourself. You may need to make a personal commitment to pray more faithfully for other people. Remember, God is pleased as you lift up others!

Thank the Father

Jesus gave us a model for prayer in Matthew 6:5–15. His example teaches us to praise God for Who He is and what He has done, to ask Him for guidance, provision, and protection, and to seek forgiveness of sin. Though there are many helpful formats for prayer, prayer should provide opportunity for adoration, praise, thanksgiving, confession of sin, and requests for self and others.

While Paul the Apostle had some serious issues to discuss with the Christians in Colossae, he began his letter in an attitude of gratitude. He sincerely expressed appreciation for their faithfulness and their partnership in ministry. He recognized three Christian virtues he noticed in them — **faith, love,** and **hope** (1:4–5).

Read these other Scripture passages where these three virtues also appear together.

Romans 5:2–5

1 Corinthians 13:13

Galatians 5:5–6

1 Thessalonians 1:3; 5:8

Hebrews 10:22–24

Why do you think *faith,* *love,* **and** *hope* **are such significant Christian virtues?**

_____

_____

_____

_____

Paul begins his prayer with thanks to the God and Father of our Lord Jesus Christ (Colossians 1:3). He then lifts up others and prays for wisdom. He concludes this first section with more gratitude. **What does Paul thank God for in Colossians 1:12?**

_____

_____

_____

_____

_____

_____

Paul's gratitude was also for the message of truth that is the gospel (Colossians 1:5–6). He acknowledged with thanks _"God's grace in the truth."_ Even in his thankfulness for Christian friends, Paul was concerned about heresy that was infiltrating the Colossian church. While grateful for their faith, he was burdened by the false teaching that had been accepted. They wanted to add rules and regulations to God's gift of grace. Nothing should be added to the gospel. We can share Paul's gratitude and concern today. Are you grateful for the many who lift up the gospel but concerned about the many who distort the truth?

Prayer was Paul's response, and prayer should be our response. In his letter to the Colossians, there is a suggested format for prayer. Do you have a format that guides your prayertime? It is helpful to be specific and structured as you pray.

One helpful format for prayer is represented by the acronym ACTS. Certainly prayer should be an active process, with the believer speaking to the Father and listening to Him. As we pray, the four letters remind us of specific ways to pray.

A—Adoration

C—Confession

T—Thanksgiving

S—Supplication

Spend time in prayer right now. Be sure to include in your prayertime some expression of adoration (praise for who He is), confession (repentance of personal sin), thanksgiving (gratitude for what He has done), and supplication (humble and earnest requests for yourself and others).

Ask for Power

Paul is quite clear in Colossians 1:9–12 about how to pray. He tells us to boldly and continuously ask for power as we pray for ourselves and for others. Specifically, Paul says we are to:

- Ask for knowledge of God's will (1:9)
  —*then you will receive Scripture understanding.*

- Ask Him to help you walk worthy of the Lord (1:10)
  —*then you will please Him, be fruitful, and grow in knowledge of God.*

- Ask to be strengthened with all power (1:11)
  —*then you will attain patience and joy.*

It is no accident that Paul prayed for the Colossians to be *"filled with the knowledge of His will in all wisdom and spiritual understanding"* (v. 9). At that time, many Christians were being filled with heresy and false doctrine. If a Christian is filled up with the truth of God and His Word, there is not room for untruth. Christians are to be filled with the knowledge of God's will as well as filled with the Holy Spirit (Ephesians 5:18). As we know God's will and seek to follow it, we will be walking worthy of Him, living a life pleasing to the Lord (Colossians 1:10). When we walk worthy, the Bible says we bear fruit (live a productive life) and grow in the knowledge of God (know His character, His will, and His ways). Through prayer and Bible study, we can!

Christians should also pray for God's power. Why do you think it is important for a Christian to pray for power?

_____

_____

_____

_____

_____

_____

How does God's power strengthen you each day? List five ways.

1. _____

2. _____

3. _____

4. _____

5. _____

Christians are to seek God's power, not for personal success, but in order to perform service for God. The believer is *"strengthened with all power"* in proportion to His power. If God is all-powerful (omnipotent), then the believer has unlimited power available for Christian living.

God's power is released through prayer! Paul had reason to praise the Lord in Colossians 1:12: *"Giving thanks to the Father, who has enabled you to share in the saints' inheritance in the light."* God has qualified us to inherit His blessings. As a result, we should lift up others, thank the Father, and ask for power. As we do, we maintain spiritual wellness.

Prescription 2 for Spiritual Wellness

"So that you may walk worthy of the Lord, fully pleasing [to Him], bearing fruit in every good work and growing in the knowledge of God" (Colossians 1:10).

Personal Spiritual Wellness

How pleased is God with your prayer life?

_____

_____

_____

_____

_____

_____

Reflect on the time you have spent with the Lord this week, then write a prayer of recommitment to please God by faithful prayer.

_____

_____

_____

_____

_____

_____

The Incomparable Christ

Colossians 1:13–23

Introduction

Who is Christ? Earlier in our study you examined Colossians 1:21–22 to answer the question *Who are you?* Now let's examine this passage to understand better the nature of Jesus Christ. The first two chapters of Colossians are considered one of the great Christological passages. Christology is the study of Christ's nature and person. Other definitive Scriptures about Christ are: John 1 and 14, Philippians 2, and Hebrews 1 and 2.

An understanding of the person of Christ is essential to a believer's faith. The careful study of Scripture clarifies who Christ is and sets the foundation for all other doctrines. Evangelical Christology accepts the two natures of Christ (God and man) without contradiction and without comparison. Colossians specifically addresses Christ as God Incarnate, Creator of the World, Head of the Church, and Reconciler of all.

Christ Is God Incarnate

Before we begin an in-depth study of this passage, read Colossians 1:13–23.

List some of the qualities identified with Christ in the verses below.

Verse 15 — _____

Verse 16 — _____

Verse 17 — _____

Verse 18 — _____

Verse 19 — _____

Verse 20 — _____

Verse 21 — _____

Verse 22 — _____

Verse 23 — _____

These verses list several qualities of Christ. He is deliverer, redeemer, forgiver, God, firstborn, creator, ruler, eternal, head of church, and reconciler among many other godly attributes.

See "A Hymn of Him" at the end of this lesson. Read it aloud to remind yourself that He is *"the Messiah, the Son of the living God"* **(Matthew 16:16).**

Colossians 1:15 clearly states that Christ is *"the image of the invisible God, the firstborn over all creation."*

What does Paul mean when he calls Christ the image of God?

_____

_____

_____

The Greek word *eikon,* which is translated "image," literally means "perfect manifestation." This word is also used when referring to likenesses placed on coins, portraits, and statues. It implies something is equal to the original. Jesus Christ is the perfect manifestation of God. He is equivalent to God. He is 100 percent God. The writer of Hebrews affirms that Christ is exactly like God:

"He is the radiance of His glory, the exact expression of His nature" (Hebrews 1:3).

Christ is also God Incarnate. That means, He is God in the flesh, 100 percent man. Therefore, we accept the two natures of Christ. He is both God and man, divine and human, infinite and finite. Christ is God, the firstborn or ruler over all creation.

These facts about Jesus Christ are the essence of evangelical Christology.

1. Christ is 100 percent God and 100 percent man (John 1:1,14).

2. God was made flesh to live among us as Christ (Philippians 2:6–7).

3. Jesus was conceived by the Holy Spirit, born of the virgin Mary (Luke 1:35).

4. Though He lived in a sinful world, Jesus lived a perfect, sinless life (Matthew 5:48).

5. Christ died on the Cross to pay the price of our sin (1 Peter 3:18).

6. His resurrection proved His deity and returned Him as a living presence with Christians (John 14:25–28).

7. Jesus reigns in heaven with God, eager to bring men to God (John 16:5–11).

Other beliefs about Jesus Christ are not biblical. Paul disputed the Colossian heresy by proclaiming Christ is God Himself. An accurate understanding of God will strengthen your personal faith and promote spiritual wellness.

Christ Is Creator of the World

The first verse of the Bible states clearly that God is the Creator of all that exists—*"in the beginning God created the heavens and the earth"* (Genesis 1:1). The first words of Scripture attribute the creation of all things to God Himself and God alone.

Take a few moments to examine Scripture to verify the creator. **What do these passages say about who created the world?**

John 1:3 _____

Colossians 1:16 _____

Hebrews 1:2 _____

God always existed, and He alone created everything. All things without exception were created through Him (John 1:3). He created all things and people for Himself (Colossians 1:16). And, God made the universe through His Son Jesus (Hebrews 1:2).

God created everything with order and purpose. Read these verses in Genesis and briefly summarize the creative work of God. Be reminded of the creative power of God.

Day 1 (Genesis 1:2–5)—He created _____

_____

Day 2 (Genesis 1:6–8)—He created _____

_____

Day 3 (Genesis 1:9–13)—He created _____

_____

Day 4 (Genesis 1:14–19) — He created _____

_____

Day 5 (Genesis 1:20–23) — He created _____

_____

Day 6 (Genesis 1:24–31) — He created _____

_____

Day 7 (Genesis 2:1–3) — He _____

_____

Paul made it very clear in Colossians 1:16 that God created every-thing. He created everything that exists for His own good plea-sure. While the gnostics believed an inferior God was responsible for creation, Paul taught that the One True God by His Son Jesus created all things. God created everything in heaven and earth, everything seen and unseen, all people and all powers. Every-thing was created by God, for His purpose and pleasure, with His involvement.

Christ Is Head of the Church

In Colossians, Paul described Christ as God, as Creator, and as *"head of the body, the church"* (1:18). Jesus Christ who is sovereign over creation is also ruler of the church. "Head" translated from the Greek word *kephale* means "authority." Jesus is the One in authority over the church, those who follow Him.

The church is a group of believers meeting together to serve the Lord and spread the gospel. It can refer to one congregation (1 Corinthians 4:17) or all Christians, everywhere, of all ages, of all times (1 Corinthians 10:32). In the Bible, "church" is not a building but a group of believers. Several biblical pictures have been given to increase our understanding of the church's role. The church is described in Scripture as the people of God (1 Peter 2:9–10), a family of God (Galatians 6:10), the bride of Christ (2 Corinthians 11:2), and the body of Christ (Colossians 1:18).

The physical body needs various parts to help it function. In the same way, the church needs different members with different gifts to serve the Lord's purpose. The head is necessary to the body's life and direction. Christ is in control of the church, its faith, and its work. The members of the body work together to help it function.

Carefully study 1 Corinthians 12:12–27. What did Paul say to the Christians in Corinth about the church?

_____

_____

_____

_____

_____

Like the physical body, the church is one body with many different parts (1 Corinthians 12:12). All believers become a part of one body and are filled with one Spirit (1 Corinthians 12:13). Every part of the body has a special purpose that is equally important and must work in unity with the other parts for the body to function properly (1 Corinthians 12:14-25). The well-being or suffering of one part impacts every part, the whole body (1 Corinthians 12:26). Believers are the body of Christ, individual members are working together as one (1 Corinthians 12:27). The metaphor of the human body is helpful in understanding the work of the church.

Jesus Christ chose to be Head of the church so that He could be involved in our daily lives. Christ who is God and Creator is also Head of the church. Paul also calls Jesus a "reconciler" (Colossians 1:20).

Christ Is Reconciler of All

Reconciliation is a prominent theme among the writings of Paul. The Christians of the early church needed to hear the message of reconciliation since there was friction among them. Christians today need to hear that same message.

Look in a dictionary for the meaning of the word *reconciliation.* **Write a definition here.**

_____

_____

_____

_____

_____

Reconciliation is restoration of unity in a relationship where alienation has taken place. While the concept is found often in the New Testament, the term *reconciliation* is found only in Paul's epistles (Romans 5:10–21; 2 Corinthians 5:18–20; Ephesians 2:16; Colossians 1:20–21). Paul confronted disputes among believers, fighting among the heathen, and separation from God in his letters. God desires peace with His children and among all His children.

Read Colossians 1:19–23 and in your Bible underline the words or phrases that answer these questions.

1. Who is the reconciler?

2. To whom are we reconciled?

3. What is the result of reconciliation?

Scripture teaches that we are reconciled by Christ through His death on the Cross (v. 22). In being reconciled to God, we can be reconciled to others. Restoration with God and others results in holy, blameless, godly living. Christ desires to be the Reconciler of all.

Have you ever been estranged from a loved one or dear friend as a result of a disagreement or sin? Tension in relationships hurt our relationship with God, with the other person, and with ourselves. When my dad was away from the Lord, our relationship was distant. Both of us suffered. When he returned to the Lord, our relationship was restored. Our reconciliation helped each of us relate more openly with God and more lovingly with each other. God desires for His children to be reconciled to Himself and to others.

Your personal understanding of the nature of Christ is essential to your own faith and is also necessary for sharing the gospel. The Baptist Faith and Message statement about "God the Son" clearly explains what Scripture teaches about Christ:

> Christ is the eternal Son of God. In His incarnation as Jesus Christ He was conceived of the Holy Spirit and born of the virgin Mary. Jesus perfectly revealed and did the will of God, taking upon Himself human nature with its demands and necessities and identifying Himself completely with mankind yet without sin. He honored the divine law by His personal obedience, and in His substitutionary death on the Cross He made provision for the redemption of men from sin. He was raised from the dead with a glorified body and appeared to His disciples as the person who was with them before His crucifixion. He ascended into heaven and is now exalted at the right hand of God where He is the One Mediator, fully God, fully man, in whose Person is effected the reconciliation between God and man. He will return in power and glory to judge the world and to consummate His redemptive mission. He now dwells in all believers as the living and ever present Lord.

Stand firm on the truth of the Word that Jesus is *"the Messiah, the Son of the living God"* (Matthew 16:16). As you stand firm in that belief, you will remain spiritually well.

Prescription 3 for Spiritual Wellness

"He is the image of the invisible God, the firstborn over all creation" (Colossians 1:15).

Personal Spiritual Wellness

Who is Christ? How does He reveal Himself to you each day? Write a list of specific ways that Christ makes Himself known to you on a daily basis.

_____

_____

_____

_____

_____

_____

_____

_____

_____

_____

A Hymn of Him
(Colossians 1:15–20)

(Section 1) 15*a*   He is the image
                         of the invisible God,

15*b*   the firstborn over all creation;

Chorus: **He is the Messiah, the Son of the
                         living God** (Matthew 16:16).

16*a*   Because by Him everything was created,

16*b*   in heaven and on earth,

16*c*   the visible and the invisible,
                         whether thrones or dominions
                         or rulers or authorities.

Chorus: **He is the Messiah, the Son of the
                         living God** (Matthew 16:16).

16*∂*   All things have been created
                         through Him and for Him.

(Section 2) 17*a*   He is before all things,

17*b*   and by Him all things hold together.

Chorus: He is the Messiah, the Son of the
                         living God (Matthew 16:16).

(Section 3) 18*a*   He is also the head
                         of the body, the church;

Chorus: **He is the Messiah, the Son of the
                         living God** (Matthew 16:16).

(Section 4)	18*b*	He is the beginning,
	18*c*	the firstborn from the dead,
	18*d*	so that He might come to have first place in everything.
Chorus:		**He is the Messiah, the Son of the living God** (Matthew 16:16).
	19	For God was pleased to have all His fullness dwell in Him.
Chorus:		**He is the Messiah, the Son of the living God** (Matthew 16:16).
	20*a*	And through Him to reconcile everything to Himself
	20*b*	by making peace through the blood of His cross—
	20*c*	whether things on earth or things in heaven.
Chorus:		**He is the Messiah, the Son of the living God** (Matthew 16:16).

Adapted from Wright, N. T. *Tyndale New Testament Commentaries: Colossians and Philemon* (Grand Rapids, Wm. B. Eerdmans Publishing Company, 1986).

Rejoice in Suffering
Colossians 1:24–29

Introduction

Paul attempted to give the Christians in Colossae what we call in this study a prescription for spiritual wellness. First, he taught them by example and instruction how to pray. Then he clarified the nature and person of Christ. Next, Paul addressed the Christian life—how to live a godly life, set apart for Him.

In Colossians 1:24–29, the Apostle Paul considered three very specific challenges that Christians experience daily. He addressed these challenges of the Christian life: human suffering, the mysteries of our faith, and the call to service.

Suffering was known to Jesus and was not unusual to Paul or to Christians of the early church. Suffering is also a reality today. In verse 24, Paul said, *"I am completing in my flesh what is lacking Christ's afflictions."* This Scripture does not mean that Christ's atonement on the Cross was incomplete or deficient. Instead, Paul acknowledged the suffering that he and believers of all ages would experience for the sake of Christ. Jesus paid the full price for our sin, and we should be willing to suffer for His cause.

In many of his writings, Paul encouraged believers to rejoice in affliction—physical, emotional, or spiritual. He tried to help them understand or accept the mysteries of their faith, and he reminded them of their role in spreading the gospel. Today, we still ask the same questions: *Why do good people suffer? Why doesn't God make Himself known clearly to His children? Will what I am doing for God make a difference?*

We Can Rejoice in Suffering

Paul wrote about suffering from his prison cell in Rome (Acts 28:16, 30). His attitude about suffering exemplifies the appropriate Christian response to hardship. Paul rejoiced in his suffering because he knew Christ had suffered greatly on his behalf and that his own suffering was for the glory of God. Christians today who are confident of their calling can rejoice in their suffering for the sake of the gospel.

Scripture provides helpful insights for the suffering saints. Read James 1:2–4 and answer this question: How should the Christian respond to suffering?

_____

_____

_____

Because of our faith in God, Christians can face the inevitable trials with courage and joy (James 1:2). Suffering, though painful, can result in spiritual maturity (James 1:3–4). In fact, there are blessings that can lead to joy as we suffer. While suffering is a challenging path to spiritual growth, no price is too high to pay for our Jesus.

Paul suggested five reasons to rejoice in suffering. Can you experience these blessings even as you suffer?

1. *Suffering brings believers closer to Christ* (Philippians 3:10). While most Christians wouldn't choose to suffer, the pain of suffering often results in deeper fellowship with God.

2. *Suffering assures the believer that she belongs to Christ* (John 15:18–19). If Jesus suffered for His faith, other believers will too. The Holy Spirit's presence in our lives during suffering also assures our salvation.

3. *Suffering brings a future reward* (Romans 8:18–25). The present sufferings on earth are insignificant in comparison to the glorious hope of eternal life.

4. *Suffering is inevitable, but it is temporary* (1 Peter 1:6). Though pain often seems to linger, for the believer, the time of suffering is fleeting since life is eternal.

5. *Suffering for the sake of the gospel should be counted a privilege* (2 Thessalonians 1:4–8). Though suffering is not pleasant; for the believer, it is a high calling. God can use our suffering for His glory.

How have you handled suffering in your life?

_____

_____

_____

What did God teach you during your trials?

_____

_____

_____

Recently one of our faculty members and his wife were struck by a car while crossing a busy street and sustained serious injuries. My friend Retia received a severe head injury and bravely fought to recover. For months, her loving husband and devoted sons cared for her during her coma and supported her through therapy. An infection ravaged her weak body, and one day shy of the four-month marker, Retia died. We all felt the loss. We all wondered why. Through this real-life crisis, God was glorified. The faith of her husband and sons was a powerful witness. In her suffering,

Retia strengthened our faith. And, now she is absent from suffering and present with the Lord. What powerful comfort to all of us!

Whether your suffering was physical, emotional, or spiritual, the Holy Spirit was present with you to strengthen, comfort, and direct you. In your trials, you had the opportunity to grow in faith and experience His power. Your life of faith was a witness to others. Just like Paul, you could glory in your suffering knowing God was honored and the pain was fleeting. The Holy Spirit comforts through suffering and teaches the truth.

We Can Understand the Mystery

God chose to reveal to Paul a mystery of the faith. *Mystery* in ancient days did not mean something eerie or suspenseful. It described a secret hidden in the past now revealed. Paul understood a profound mystery—the mystery that the gospel was for all people. That revelation was revolutionary for Paul, a Jew and a Pharisee. In addition, it was a mystery to Paul that God would call him to minister to the Gentiles. God chooses to reveal Himself and His mystery to the saints.

Who are the saints to whom God reveals His mystery?

_____

_____

_____

What are the results of that mystery? *(See Colossians 1:26–27.)*

_____

_____

_____

The mystery of the gospel was revealed to the saints—all who accepted Jesus as Lord and Savior (Philippians 4:21). This revelation brings to all the hope of glory (Colossians 1:26–27). God does choose to reveal many truths to His children. However, some mysteries remain unknown.

Read the following statements about the mystery of our faith, and determine if they are true or false. Circle T for true statements and F for false statements. You may need to check the Scripture reference for accuracy.

T   F   1. God reveals some things to no one (Deuteronomy 29:29).

T   F   2. Certain people learn some mysteries of God (Psalm 25:14).

T   F   3. The New Testament reveals some mysteries of the Old Testament (Colossians 1:26).

T   F   4. The mysteries of God are revealed only to believers (1 Corinthians 2:7–16).

T   F   5. Men do not discover the mysteries, God reveals them (Colossians 1:27).

All of these statements are truths about the mysteries of the faith. Is there still mystery in your faith? Are there things about God you still don't understand? In your own words, try to explain those mysteries.

_____

_____

_____

_____

_____

_____

_____

_____

_____

Jesus Himself talked about the secrets or mysteries of the faith. In Matthew 13:10–17, the Great Teacher explained to His disciples why He taught in parables (earthly stories with a heavenly meaning.) He said, *"Because the secrets of the kingdom of heaven have been given for you to know, but it has not been given to them"* (v. 11). He explained biblical truths to His followers, though the mystery remained for those who did not know Him. In Paul's day and today, Jesus is revealing Himself and His ways to us.

While we will not fully understand the Father until we are with Him in Heaven, He promises that we will understand the most important mystery—the mystery of the ages that Paul faced. Christ in you is the hope of glory (Colossians 1:27). His message of hope and salvation is for all. That truth should motivate all believers to strive for the gospel. God chose to reveal that mystery to His children—to you!

We Can Strive for the Gospel

Why should we work so hard for the gospel? Colossians 1:25 answers that question definitively. We are to work for the gospel because we are called to minister, we need to be good stewards of God's gifts, and we must fulfill the Word of God. A call to ministry is a very serious matter. God calls for a purpose—to accomplish His purpose here on earth.

Have you been called by God to work for Him?

_____

_____

_____

Explain your call.

_____

_____

_____

_____

_____

_____

Paul became a minister (Colossians 1:23, 25), a high calling from God to spread the gospel to all people. He was passionate about his call. In 1 Corinthians 9:16, Paul sincerely proclaimed, *"For if I preach the gospel, I have no reason to boast, because an obligation is placed on me. And woe to me if I do not preach the gospel!"*

Pray for that same passion about God's calling in your life.

I learned about God's calling to ministry early in my life. When I was eight, my dad surrendered to the ministry and began seminary for training. When I was 15, I personally surrendered to the ministry. In college, I met and fell in love with my husband who was called to the ministry. My dad and my husband both have specific calls to evangelism. So, I fully understand that the call to ministry is a high calling with a single purpose—to spread the gospel to all people. Like Paul, I say: *"Woe to me if I do not spread the gospel!"*

Christians are to be good stewards of their calling. We don't own the gospel. The gospel is the message of God. We have the responsibility of managing the gospel. Since He chose to reveal His mystery to us and since He has called us, we are obliged to share His gospel with others. Are you a good steward of the gospel?

When did you last share your faith with an unbeliever?

_____

_____

_____

_____

_____

_____

As you record your response to that personal question, ask God to make you a faithful steward of the gospel.

Let's examine a final reason for Christians to strive for the gospel. The Bible challenges us to spread the gospel. Every believer chooses to obey or disobey God as we choose whether or not to strive for the gospel. In Colossians 1:28, Paul is specific in giving Christians instructions about how to spread the gospel.

Carefully read and reread that verse and make your gospel "to do" list below.

The Christian's To-Do List (Colossians 1:28)

1. _____

2. _____

3. _____

Christians are to proclaim Him, striving for the gospel daily. We must warn everyone, teach everyone, and present everyone perfect in Christ. That's a tall order! That's a big job! But Colossians tells us how to do it. Live a godly life, work at the task of witnessing, and depend on God's power (Colossians 1:29). Even the challenge of spreading the gospel to all people can be accomplished by the faithful labor of believers and the mighty power of God. As you toil for Him, rejoice! Rejoice in your suffering, rejoice in the mystery, and rejoice in your calling!

Prescription 4 for Spiritual Wellness

"I labor for this, striving with His strength that works powerfully in me"
(Colossians 1:29).

Personal Spiritual Wellness

In the Bible paraphrase, *The Message*, Paul challenges Christians: *"We preach Christ...that's what I'm working so hard at day after day, year after year, doing my best with the energy God so generously gives me"* (Colossians 1:28, 29 *The Message*).

What are you using your energy to proclaim? Write your own paraphrase of Colossians 1:28–29 here.

_____

_____

_____

_____

_____

_____

_____

_____

_____

_____

Lesson 5
Built Up in Christ
Colossians 2:1–15

Introduction

Bodybuilding is considered by many to be a sport. But is it really a sport? A sport is physical activity or athletic recreation. In bodybuilding, men and women work hard to build and flex muscles, but what do they actually do with their strength? Some stand before judges and audiences in skimpy swimsuits posing their oiled bodies and their rippling muscles. They do not lift a weight, run a race, or win a game. They simply display their bodies and look strong.

Christ calls us to be built up in Him not just to look strong but to lift the weights of adversity, run the race of life with endurance, and win the game He sets before us. In Colossians 2:6–7, Paul challenges Christians to be *"rooted and built up in Him."* The only reason for our spiritual strength is to serve the Lord and spread His gospel.

The Christian life should be more like a relay race; each believer, trained in the faith, should pass on the gospel with much haste to another person. Paul often wrote in his letters about running the race. In Philippians 3:14, he identifies the goal of a Christian's race — *"God's heavenly call in Christ Jesus."*

Read Philippians 3:12–14 and record some of Paul's teachings about how Christians should run the race.

_____

_____

_____

_____

_____

_____

Are you running the race of faith? Are you passing the torch of the gospel? Are you winning the race of life? Make a commitment to be rooted in Christ, built up in Him, and established in Him so that you can walk in Him each day.

Rooted in Him

After his brief digression about suffering, Paul returned to his theme of Christ and the mystery of the gospel. He struggled as he walked with people in the faith and thought of the friends he had never met in the Lycus River Valley. Paul reflected on the Christians in the towns of Laodicea and Hierapolis, as well as Colossae, and hoped they would circulate his letter among their churches. He was passionate in his concern and practical in his counsel. Paul's desire was for the Christians to be "rooted in Christ" like a tree planted in good soil and growing in strength.

Believers are to be rooted in a person not a philosophy. While people in our world today seem willing to follow any thought or practice espoused by the world, Christians should only believe in the person of Jesus Christ. Paul deeply desired for Christians to place their faith in God and rooted in His Word. Instead, many were believing the false teachings of Gnosticism (the philosophy that knowledge leads to salvation). To be rooted firmly in faith, believers must understand the mystery—there is one God for all and one way to salvation through Jesus Christ our Lord.

Read Colossians 2:1–7. How many verbs can you identify? What do these action words teach about growing a strong faith?

know (v. 1) _____

be encouraged (v. 2) _____

be joined together (v. 2) _____

say (v. 4) _____

receive (v. 6) _____

walk (v. 6) _____

It was important to Paul that the Christians of his day _know_ his concern for them and _know_ the truth (v. 1). He wanted to _encourage_ their hearts as his letters continue to _encourage_ us today (v. 2). He wanted them to _be joined_ together in love, united as one and living harmoniously (v. 2). Paul spoke truth _saying_ they had been deceived by the persuasive arguments of the heretics (v. 4). Instead, the Christians in Colossae should _receive_ Christ Jesus alone, not following other gods (v. 6). And, they should _walk_ in Christ, not in themselves or the world (v. 6). His teachings provide solid doctrine for us today.

When my dad left the Lord, my strong faith in God saw me through the heartbreak. Though I loved my dad, my faith was not in him. If we place our trust in a person or a philosophy, we will easily be shaken in trying times. But, if our faith is planted firmly in Christ, our salvation is sure even when our life is uncertain.

If believers are to grow strong in the faith, we must walk daily in Christ—continuing to believe the truth about Him. Just as a tree sinks its roots deeply in the rich soil, believers must root themselves deeply in Christ. Salvation begins the planting process and a relationship with Christ nourishes spiritual growth and produces fruit. Keep your life deeply rooted in Him!

Built Up in Him

Paul also prayed that the Colossians would be _"built up in Him."_ He suggested an architectural picture of the Christian building her faith on the firm foundation of Christ. A Christian must be spiritually strong.

For physical well-being, a woman must eat a balanced diet and exercise regularly. That daily regimen will build up or strengthen the body physically. Pamela Smith said, "Proper nutrition without exercise is like a car without tires—the body may look good, but it won't go anywhere!" Spiritual well-being is the same. A believer must learn faith in Christ and abound in it in order to be spiritually strong (see Colossians 2:7).

When a person wants to lose weight, she is tempted to take shortcuts by trying a crash diet or taking diet pills. Though she may lose weight quickly, she rarely sustains the weight loss. Medical experts recommend a combination of proper nutrition and exercise to reduce weight gradually. Another result is a healthier lifestyle. Some believers are also tempted to accept false teachings and believe deceptive doctrine. Read Colossians 2:8–10. Paul strongly warned believers not to settle for less than the truth.

Write Paul's warning in Colossians 2:8 in your own words.

_____

_____

_____

_____

_____

_____

To be built up spiritually, Christians must feed on the Word of God and walk in the Spirit. We must be properly nourished—filling ourselves with God's nature (v. 9) and putting off the sins of the flesh (v. 11). We must exercise regularly, walking in Him daily through Bible study, prayer, and ministry (v. 6). As Christians persevere in our spiritual nutrition and fitness, we grow in strength and endurance.

Only in Christ does the fullness of God dwell (Colossians 2:9–10). In the musical _God with Us_, the narrator recites the names of God given in the Bible from Genesis to Revelation. It is thrilling to hear the 66 names of God, from _"The Ram at Abraham's altar"_ in

Genesis to *"The King of kings and Lord of lords"* in Revelation. In the Book of Colossians, God is called *"fullness of the God's nature dwells bodily""* (Colossians 2:9). Knowing who God is and how He works in lives is essential to faith. Only through a knowledge of God and a steadfast walk in faith is a believer complete (Colossians 2:10). God the Creator, who revealed Himself to us in His Son Jesus Christ and the Holy Spirit, dwells in every believer and builds us up.

Without God, a person is incomplete. Without God, there is emptiness. Without God, there is a piece missing, a lack of strength. The philosopher and scientist Blaise Pascal said, "There is a God-shaped vacuum in every heart." St. Augustine prayed, "Our hearts are restless until they find rest in thee." My husband, Dr. Chuck Kelley says, "Jesus is the missing piece to the puzzle of our soul." Each statement clearly challenges all people to fill their emptiness with Jesus, to find rest in Him, and to be complete in Him. Ephesians 6:10 says, *"Be strong in the Lord, and in the power of His might"* (KJV). Therefore, put your faith in Him and let Him build you up.

Established in Him

To be strong in the Lord, believers must be rooted in Him, built up in Him, and established in Him. Paul gave specific instructions in Colossians 2:7, be *"established in the faith."* What does it mean to be established? The dictionary defines the verb *establish* in several ways: *"to make stable, make firm, settle; to order, ordain or enact permanently."* One of those definitions relates directly to Paul's instruction in Colossians 2:11–15. Carefully read this passage. Paul exhorted believers to establish their faith, to be schooled rightly in the truth. One evidence of sound doctrine was the ordinance of baptism.

An ordinance is a symbolic act set into practice by Jesus Christ. In Colossians 2:11, Paul first explained about salvation. We learn that salvation is not just for the Jew who was physically circumcised. Salvation by faith in Jesus Christ is for all and results in a spiritual circumcision—freedom from the power of the flesh. Then Paul described New Testament baptism. Baptism is for believers and symbolizes the death and resurrection of Jesus, while also depicting the death of *the old person* and the resurrection of *a new person* (Colossians 3:9–10). Though baptism is not necessary for salvation, it is an act of obedience that demonstrates our faith.

When each of my nephews was baptized after making a public profession of faith, we celebrated. We had a family party for this spiritual birthday. My husband and I gave each of them a leather Bible with their name engraved on it. Every family member present marked their favorite Scripture in the new convert's Bible. We wanted their baptismal experience to be memorable. Baptism is important for believers. It affirms faith personally and expresses the gospel publicly. A believer's baptism should be celebrated.

Can you think of ways to make the ordinance of baptism special to a new convert? List a few suggestions here.

_____

_____

_____

_____

_____

_____

The point is this: baptism is to be a public display of the personal faith of a believer. It can be an effective way to explain the gospel to the lost.

Paul concluded this section in the second chapter of Colossians with a description of forgiveness. The forgiveness of Jesus Christ is different from human forgiveness.

What do these phrases in Colossians 2 teach about forgiveness of sin?

- *"forgave all our trespasses"* (v. 13):

_____

_____

_____

_____

_____

- *"erased the certificate of debt"* (v. 14):

_____

_____

_____

_____

_____

- *"taken it out of the way by nailing it to the cross"* (v. 14):

_____

_____

_____

_____

While our debt of sin resulted from violation of the law of God, Jesus Christ completely paid the price for our sin (v. 13). He canceled our debt (v. 14). He took away our sin completely when He nailed it to the Cross (v. 14). Only when a believer understands the mystery of salvation does she have the whole picture.

Paul provided a beautiful biblical picture that can speak to women today: "I want their hearts to be encouraged and be knitted together in love" (Colossians 2:2, NKJV). He encouraged believers to be "knit together with love." A knitted garment is such a gift of love. Knitters invest many hours to create a beautiful pattern from strings of yarn. Love is woven into each stitch.

However, we do not fully appreciate the special work of art until the project is complete. Then, we understand completely, and the uncertainty is revealed. As believers, our pieces of life are knitted together with love. But, the total picture is not complete unless the believer is rooted in Him, built up in Him, and established in Him.

Prescription 5 for Spiritual Wellness

"Therefore as you have received Christ Jesus the Lord, walk in Him"
(Colossians 2:6).

Personal Spiritual Wellness

How strongly are you built up in Christ? Examine your spiritual strength in the same way a doctor might examine your physical strength. How many pounds are you lifting daily in your spiritual life? Use a scale of 1 to 10, with 10 being the heaviest weight. Be honest in your estimation.

Bible study — _____ lbs.

Prayer — _____ lbs.

Witnessing — _____ lbs.

Service — _____ lbs.

Are you a weakling or a superwoman?

_____

What is your new spiritual fitness program?

_____

_____

_____

_____

Lesson 6
Spiritual Nutrition
Colossians 2:16–23

Introduction

Have you ever experienced the "diet principle?" Simply stated it is the physical and psychological phenomenon of increased hunger when a diet is begun. Isn't that true? If you decide to lose weight, you immediately desire to eat more food. Negative reinforcement seems to increase the appetite. While hard to explain, its reality is evident. The more you try not to eat, the more you want to eat.

While good nutrition is the goal, most people struggle to maintain a healthy diet. For Christians who typically define fellowship with food, the battle of the bulge is a recurring challenge. The Bible teaches about care of the body as well as care of the soul. Many biblical principles apply to physical diet and spiritual diet—avoid what is unhealthy, avoid what is a fad diet or false teaching, and partake of what is healthy. The Christians in Colossae were struggling with spiritual nutrition as we do today.

In Paul's time, the roots of Gnosticism and Jewish legalism were prevalent. The Christians in Colossae were adding unhealthy practices to their faith. False teaching limited knowledge to the spiritual elite and added works to salvation by faith. Regulations and practices developed to measure spirituality and added to the Christian belief that Christ alone is sufficient for salvation.

Christ came to fulfill the law and to provide salvation through faith alone. Therefore, our faith is not dependent on adherence to rules and regulations but on personal belief in Jesus Christ as Savior. For the Christian, all her cravings can be met in Christ. Salvation by faith should satisfy the believer's appetite.

Like the Christians in Paul's day, we must maintain a healthy spiritual diet—taking in only what is truth and good for us, rejecting what is false and bad for us. Let's examine this passage from the perspective of an unhealthy diet, a fad diet, and a healthy diet spiritually.

The Unhealthy Diet

Jewish legalists and those involved in Gnostic thought added works to faith. They insisted on behavioral practices to ensure salvation. Religious additives, like their laws and observances, are just as unhealthy spiritually as food additives are dangerous physically. An additive is any substance added to another to achieve a desired effect. The additives in food not only take away from the natural flavor, but they add substances that are unnatural and often harmful to the body. Spiritual additives in turn take away from the pure truth and add unnecessary human effort.

Carefully read Colossians 2:16–23. These verses refer to four specific practices of some people in Colossae. After you read the description of each false teaching, record a Scripture verse or verses in this passage that address that particular teaching.

1. **Observation of days**—In addition to food regulations, some of the Colossians identified lists of days that belonged to God. They observed yearly feasts, monthly new moons, and weekly Sabbaths with elaborate ritual. The focus was on adherence to the ritual not worship of God.

What verse in this passage warns about this practice?

_____

2. **Asceticism**—Some believed that all matter is essentially evil, and they went to extremes to limit what a person ate or drank. Extensive regulations were developed to list clean and unclean foods. They practiced legalistic obedience to the letter of the law.

What verses in Colossians 2:16–23 address this practice?

_____

3. **Worship of angels** — With their strong belief in angels and the work of many spiritual intermediaries, many people began to worship angels in the same way they worshiped God. Paul reminded the Colossian Christians that worship was reserved for God and Jesus Christ alone. While angels do minister to believers, they are only messengers of God. They are not God and are not worthy of worship (Hebrews 1:14).

What verses specifically discuss this practice?

_____

4. **Special visions** — Some people believed that divine knowledge was limited to only the elite intellectuals. Therefore, it was common for certain individuals to boast about special revelations and interpretive power. These mystics spoke of visions that they felt the ordinary man couldn't see or understand. They prided themselves in a false godliness. Paul warned the Christians in Colossae about these false teachers.

What verse in this passage records his warning about this practice?

_____

Paul responded firmly to heresy in the Colossian church. He clearly stated that salvation is through faith in Jesus Christ alone (Colossians 1:4), and works are not necessary for salvation but are evidence of salvation (Colossians 3:12–14). In Colossians 2, Paul addresses four false practices. Some Christians in Colossae criticized those who did not observe certain religious practices such as dietary laws and special days (vv. 2:16–17). Others were criticized for ascetic practices and the worship of angels (v. 18). Others believed special visions from God were limited to the spiritually elite (v. 18). Paul warned Christians who had died to Christ not to submit also to the regulations of the world.

As Christians today, we struggle with dying to self and living for Christ—with living in the world but not belonging to the world (Colossians 2:20). Many Christians appear to follow Christ (attending church, helping those in need, speaking about Him), while they also enjoy what the world has to offer (material possessions, sensual pleasures, worldly priorities). Because of our sinful human nature, this tension between the spirit and the flesh will always exist. Paul tried to explain to the Colossians and to us that mature Christians trust in God alone and don't add human practices to their faith. These false teachings constitute an unhealthy diet.

The Fad Diet

Throughout history, people have been unhealthy or unbalanced personally and sought quick fixes to remedy their problems. We follow any personality who seems to have the answer. Therefore, we often follow fad and trendy spokesmen. And, in the process, we elevate humans to a pedestal rather than clinging to God alone as divine. It is easier for some to trust the words of an apparently inspired person who can be seen and touched than to have faith in an invisible though ever-present God and His inspired Word, the Bible.

The Gnostics followed false prophets who thought they were the only ones to receive wisdom from God. Paul reminded the Christians that God speaks directly to His children. He warned them about letting spiritual leaders dictate behavior and cast judgment (Colossians 2:16–18). We need to be warned today.

There are definite dangers in listening to the advice of others instead of the wisdom of God. Believers have direct access to God through His Word and the work of the Holy Spirit. But instead, we listen to human instruction as the inerrant word. We are blessed today with many excellent Christian resources—inspirational books and Bible studies. It seems easier for most Christians to read what others have to say than to hear directly from the Lord. Be warned that *these are a shadow of what was to come; the substance is the Messiah*" (Colossians 2:17). Why settle for second-hand or second-rate when you can have truth directly from God Himself!

Richard Simmons built a profession as a diet guru some years ago. His energetic exercise programs and highly regulated diet plans have helped many people lose weight. However, many of his followers credit him personally for their weight loss and not the exercise program or proper nutrition. Often people find it easier to follow people than to follow God.

There is also a risk in following spiritual gurus. Some cults today exercise more faith in an individual than faith in God. The leader's personal experience may be assigned universal meaning. Therefore, followers blindly obey the guru and become a literal clone. This is an extreme example of "the guru principle." However, many Christians today who love a pastor or Bible study teacher may listen more obediently to that person than they do to the Word of God. Paul challenges Christians to *"hold on to the head"* (Colossians 2:19). The Head of the Church is Jesus Christ. He is the one we should follow.

While Christians must avoid following human gurus, the importance of Christian examples cannot be overlooked. In her book, *A Garden Path to Mentoring*, Esther Burroughs defines mentoring as "pouring your love for God into another." Numerous Scriptures teach the importance of mentoring (for example, Titus 2:1–5). To be a godly mentor you must first understand the meaning of mentor.

Contrast the difference between a guru and a mentor.

_____

_____

_____

_____

_____

_____

A *guru* is one regarded with great wisdom, knowledge, and authority—a self-proclaimed higher authority. While a *mentor* is a trusted friend, counselor, or teacher—usually a more experienced person. A guru implies authority in ranks; a mentor connotes a peer relationship. Christians need peers to guide them through life though only Christ should be the authority in faith.

In a personal tribute in *A Garden Path to Mentoring*, Melody Burroughs Reid said about her mother, "She is my best friend, my hero, and my mentor, always pointing me in the direction of Jesus Christ." The key difference is that while a human guru draws attention to self, a spiritual mentor points a person to Jesus.

Are there people in your life who have influenced you toward godliness? Are you a godly mentor for other followers of Christ? Thank God for the positive influence of these godly mentors, but be careful not to focus so much on them that you don't see Christ. The Bible clearly teaches of the importance of Christian role models, though Christ should always be our perfect model.

An important lesson can be learned from the guru principle. While others can be an example of godly living, Christ alone is our model of righteousness. Beware of following others rather than imitating Christ! Don't let fad teachings or persuasive people distract you from the truth of God and His Word. As a believer, you are responsible for your own spirituality. While other Christians may serve as mentors to you, no one can relate to God for you.

The Healthy Diet

In this final section of Colossians 2, Paul warned the Colossians about adding regulations to their faith and about following spiritual gurus. Those who followed these practices were spiritually unhealthy. They were not a part of the work of Christ, and they were not growing in their faith. They were guilty of several false teachings. First, they understood only half-truths (Colossians 2:16–23). Their faith was dependent only on observance of regulations, not personal relationship with Christ. Second, they practiced false humility (Colossians 2:18, 23). They believed few people were worthy of access to God. Christianity professes a salvation for all. Third, they exhibited sinful pride (Colossians 2:18, 23). They boasted of spiritual knowledge and intellectual elitism. And fourth, they supported unnecessary slavery to ritual and routine (Colossians 2:20, 23). The adherence to strict rules and regulations imposes bondage and negates freedom in Christ. Christ's death on the Cross provided liberty for all believers, freedom from the power and penalty of sin.

What regulations and rules are you following that rob you of your freedom in Christ?

1. _____

2. _____

3. _____

4. _____

5. _____

Christians have the privilege of a *relationship* with Christ and are not bound by the *regulations* of man. While unhealthy spiritual practices are to be avoided, healthy lifestyles are to be developed. Christians must maintain a healthy spiritual diet—practices that will help them grow and mature in the Lord.

A healthy diet physically includes essential foods in suggested amounts daily. The food pyramid makes these recommendations for the daily adult diet: 6 or more servings of bread and cereal; 3–5 servings of vegetables; 2–4 servings of fruit; 2 servings of dairy products; 2 servings of meat; and occasional fats, oils, and sweets. Informed individuals know the components of a balanced physical diet though they may struggle to follow it faithfully. If you do maintain a balanced diet, better health and increased energy will most likely result.

What about your spiritual diet? What practices do you follow daily to promote your spiritual growth? List on the next page each spiritual discipline you practice and in what dose or length of time.

Discipline	Dose
_____	_____
_____	_____
_____	_____
_____	_____
_____	_____
_____	_____

As a Christian, you will constantly struggle to maintain healthy spiritual nutrition. You must make renewed commitments to practice spiritual disciplines daily in order to grow spiritually and prevent spiritual decline.

Let these Spiritual Diet Do's and Don'ts from Colossians 2:16–23 guide your life.

v. 16   DON'T let anyone judge you on what you eat.
DO remember that your judge is Jesus.

v. 17   DON'T settle for less than Jesus.
DO remember that the substance is Jesus.

v. 18   DON'T be disqualified for your reward.
DO follow God faithfully and receive your reward.

v. 19   DON'T forget the Head.
DO be a part of the whole body.

v. 20   DON'T live for the world.
DO live for Christ.

v. 20 DON'T be ruled by regulations.
       DO believe in God's grace.

v. 21 DON'T focus on the perishable (temporary).
       DO focus on the imperishable (lasting-eternal).

v. 22 DON'T believe false teachings.
       DO believe only the truth of God's Word.

Paul desperately desired for the Christians in Colossae to be healthy spiritually and grow in their faith. He discussed spiritual nutrition in Colossians 2. He warned the Christians then and us today to avoid an unhealthy diet, beware of fad diets, and maintain a healthy diet spiritually. When you pay the price for proper nutrition, you will promote good spiritual health.

Prescription 6 for Spiritual Wellness

"If you died with Christ to the elemental forces of this world, why do you live as if you still belonged to the world? Why do you submit to regulations" (Colossians 2:20).

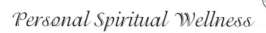

Personal Spiritual Wellness

Carefully read Colossians 2:20. Then read Paul's similar statement
of faith in Galatians 2:18–21. Now write the meaning of Colossians
2:20 in your own words.

_____

_____

_____

_____

_____

Healthy Christian Living

Colossians 3:1–11

Introduction

A wide discrepancy developed between legalistic Jewish ritual and undisciplined behavior, which God freely forgives. On the one hand, false teachers taught strict adherence to the letter of the law while new Christians believed in Christ's forgiveness of all sin. A chasm developed separating the works-based view of salvation (Colossians 2:20) from the Christians' understanding of salvation by faith (Colossians 3:2). Dangers are inherent in both. Some in Colossae began to worry about salvation based on their effort alone. The Christians expressed little concern about their behavior since sins are forgiven by God. The Scripture warns about both perspectives.

Paul confronted those adhering to works-based salvation of the Gnostics in Colossians 2 when he said, *"If you died with Christ to the elemental forces of this world, why do you live as if you still belonged to the world? Why do you submit to regulations"* (v. 20). However, he quickly warned believers in chapter 3 about carnal behavior (see vv. 1–11). While salvation comes by faith alone, godly living is a natural result of salvation. The focus of Colossians is on a personal relationship with God, not a perfect practice of the law.

Most Christians would worry themselves to death if their own actions determined their salvation. Worry is not conducive to good physical health, and it undermines spiritual health as well. In another letter, Paul discussed anxiety. *"Don't worry about anything, but in everything, through prayer and petition with thanksgiving, let your requests be made known to God"* (Philippians 4:6). He warned Christians not to worry, because worrying doesn't help. God's work, not our worry, makes a difference!

Jesus Christ pleaded with His disciples not to worry. Three times in Matthew 6:25–34, He said, *"Do not worry."* He assured them and He assures us that He will provide for all our needs, even our greatest need—salvation. Worry takes the focus off of Christ and His ample provision for all of our needs. In truth, worry waters down our faith. Our faith is dependent on God's love for us, not our own actions.

While our actions don't determine our salvation, our behavior is important to God. He promises to forgive sin, but He rejoices when He observes godly living. **Read Colossians 3:1–11 to understand Christ's desire for our healthy Christian living.** As Paul begins, he reiterates a strong conviction, *"So if you have been raised with the Messiah, seek what is above, where the Messiah is, seated at the right hand of God"* (Colossians 3:1). If you are saved, you are a new creation and should live for Christ. Then your life should be *consistent, real,* and *godly.*

Be Consistent

"So if you're serious about living this new resurrection life with Christ, act like it" (Colossians 3:1 *The Message*). Paul is very direct when he confronts the Colossian Christians. If you are a Christian, act like it! The greatest challenge facing Christians today is living out our faith. It is essential for the Christian's lifestyle to be consistent with the Christian faith and different from the world. Living a consistent life of Christlikeness day after day is also important.

In the late 1800s, a godly Christian woman named Hannah Whitall Smith became concerned about the inconsistencies in the lives of professed Christians. She expressed her concern in the book, *The Christian's Secret to a Happy Life*. This same concern could be voiced today. "The standard of practical holy living has been so low among Christians that the least degree of real devotedness of life and walk is looked upon with surprise … by a large portion of the Church. And, for the most part, the followers of Jesus Christ are satisfied with a life so conformed to the world, and so like it in almost every respect, that, to a casual observer, no difference is discernible" (p. 130).

Are you *satisfied* with your life as it is, or do you want to be *set apart* from the world by your godly lifestyle? Read Colossians 3:1–11 then fill in the blanks below.

verse 1 —*seek* _____

verse 2 —*set your minds* _____

verse 5 —*put to death* _____

How are you living your life consistently with these biblical teachings?

_____

_____

_____

_____

_____

_____

Several years ago, my husband was leading an evangelism training conference in Las Vegas, Nevada. As he waited at the airport to depart the "gambling capital of the world," he was tempted to try out a slot machine situated right there at his airport gate. He was simply curious and initially thought it would be OK to gamble just once. But then the Lord convicted him to live out his faith—to practice what he preached. So he didn't put the quarter in the machine. As he boarded the plane, a man from the church said, "Hi, Preacher. I've been watching you to see if you would gamble when you thought nobody was looking." His testimony would have been tarnished if his life hadn't been consistent with his faith. His life choice was consistent with biblical teachings.

How can you be consistent in your Christian living? In Colossians 3:1: Paul says, *"seek what is above."* In our lives, we should always put God and His ways before our own. Then in Colossians 3:2, he states: *"Set your mind on what is above, not on what is on the earth."* Our minds should be focused only on God and the truth of His Word. In Colossians 3:5, he challenges us: *"Put to death whatever in you is worldly."* To be a genuine believer, we must die to our old self.

The Lord truly desires for us to be consistent in living out our faith. "Walk the talk" is a key prescription to healthy Christian living. Live out your faith.

Be Real

It is important to the Christian's witness for her lifestyle to be consistent with her faith. It is also essential for the Christian to be real—genuine, honest, truthful. When God changes a person's heart, He creates a new person. The old person dies and the "real person" is created in the image of God. In Colossians 3:5, Paul's advice to Christians is to die to your old self. Christians are not to literally kill themselves but continually extinguish evil desires or lusts.

In the following two verses, Paul interrupted the list of sins to explain why changing from our sinful ways and becoming a new creation is so essential. First, we are reminded that sin brings God's judgment. Colossians 3:6 says, *"Because of these, God's wrath comes on the disobedient."* Wrath is God's intentional reaction to sin.

What do these verses teach about the wrath of God?

John 3:36 _____

_____

Romans 1:18 _____

_____

Romans 2:5 _____

_____

1 Thessalonians 1:10 _____

_____

Wrath is strong vengeance or angry indignation. Even a loving God hates sin and releases His wrath. According to Scripture, the wrath of God remains on those who refuse to believe (John 3:36). God's wrath is revealed against all godless and unrighteous people (Romans 1:18). A person with a hardness of heart and unrepentant spirit, in time, will experience the wrath of God (Romans 2:5). When a person accepts Christ and lives in new Christlikeness, Jesus rescues the person from impending wrath (1 Thessalonians 1:10). The reality of God's wrath should motivate believers to live a real life in Christ.

What do you know personally about the wrath of God?

_____

_____

_____

_____

_____

_____

A second reason for believers to put sin to death (Colossians 3:5) is that sin is a part of the believer's past. After conversion, sinfulness is no longer acceptable. It becomes deception when an individual professes faith and lives a sinful life. That ungodly lifestyle was a part of the old self, the life without Christ

(Colossians 3:7). To continue in sin after salvation is to live a lie, to be deceptive to the world.

Being a fake, pretending, or keeping up a facade is difficult. My husband and I visited a college friend several years after graduation. As she discussed her involvement in church (singing in the choir, teaching Sunday School), we were thrilled with her apparent strong faith. Only later did we learn that she was having an affair with a married man in the church. She had not given us the full picture. In fact, she had been deceptive and dishonest. She had not died to her sinful ways.

Don't live a lie! Be real. Put sin to death; put sin behind; and be who God created you to be. Act out your faith and live a healthy Christian life.

Be Godly

In the final verses of Colossians 3:1–11, Paul contrasts the "old man" and the "new man." He clearly exhorts believers to put *off* the sinful ways of the old man and put *on* the godly ways of the new man. The characteristics of these lives are in sharp contrast.

Carefully read verses 8 through 14. List below the behaviors to be "put off" and those to be "put on" by the believer.

Put Off (Colossians 3:8–9)   Put On (Colossians 3:12–14)

_____   _____

_____   _____

_____   _____

_____   _____

_____   _____

_____   _____

_____   _____

The old sinful life is characterized by anger, wrath, malice, slander, filthy language, and lying which should be behaviors of the past (Colossians 3:8–9). On the other hand, the new life in Christ should be characterized by compassion, kindness, humility, gentleness, patience, acceptance, forgiveness, and love, which should be pursued (Colossians 3:12–14).

Paul also contrasted the life of the old man and the new man in Galatians 5. In verses 19–21, he tells Christians to avoid deeds of the flesh such as adultery, idolatry, jealousy, and heresy. In verses 22 and 23, he calls believers to a new life evidenced by the fruit of the Holy Spirit (love, joy, peace, patience, kindness, goodness, faithfulness, gentleness, and self-control). A healthy Christian is a holy Christian—a believer living a godly life. If your desire is to maintain spiritual wellness, your faith must be consistent, real, and godly.

In reflecting on Colossians 3:1–11, there are several helpful hints for healthy Christian living.

Refer to the specific Scriptures and fill in the blanks to complete each statement.

1. Seek _____(3:1).

2. Set your mind on _____(3:2).

3. Put to death _____(3:5).

4. Be renewed in _____(3:10).

This passage gives us a powerful prescription for spiritual wellness—a plan for healthy Christian living.

Prescription 7 for Spiritual Wellness

"Set your minds on what is above, not on what is on the earth"
(Colossians 3:2).

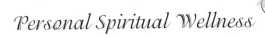

Personal Spiritual Wellness

Is your daily life an accurate reflection of your faith? Are you consistent in your walk and your talk? Write a sentence to describe how your faith in God looks to others.

_____

_____

_____

_____

_____

Are there changes you need to make in your life to be a healthy Christian?

_____

_____

_____

_____

_____

Renew your commitment to live a life that is consistent, real, and godly.

Dress for Success
Colossians 3:12–17

Introduction

While God is most concerned about inner beauty, women are often more interested in outer beauty. We spend hours each day trying to improve our appearance. Many of us carefully shop for just the right clothing. Our wardrobe in many ways is a reflection of who we are.

What if you were going on a trip and could only pack eight items of clothing. What eight pieces of clothing would you choose to take? List those essential garments.

1. _____

2. _____

3. _____

4. _____

5. _____

6. _____

7. _____

8. _____

Women today do struggle when selecting a wardrobe. When we did this activity in our women's Bible study, participants asked questions before we could answer others. Where were we going?

How long would we be gone? Does underwear count as a piece of clothing? Everyone had serious considerations about clothing. While we may have different styles and preferences in clothing, most of us would agree that a travel wardrobe would include basic items with flexibility and variety. God desires for us to be just as conscientious about our spiritual wardrobe as we are about our personal one.

A Personal Wardrobe

What is hanging in your closet right now? I am trying to find time to clean out my closet. It seems this is a never-ending task. There are clothes that no longer fit or are no longer in style. Some clothes need mending, and some outfits need updating. I strive to have in my closet all the basic clothing items I need to be properly dressed for every season and every occasion because I always want to look my best.

A recent women's clothing catalog included helpful suggestions about how to dress for success. It suggested an eight-piece wardrobe guaranteed appropriate for every occasion. I quickly went to my closet for an inventory and found my wardrobe lacking in several areas. Do you have these eight basic items of clothing in your closet?

1. A classic jacket

2. A basic dress

3. Neutral pants

4. A white shirt

5. A flattering skirt

6. A colorful scarf

7. Comfortable shoes

8. A sturdy purse

If we spend so much time worrying about our personal wardrobe, shouldn't we spend even more time preparing our spiritual wardrobe? **Read Colossians 3:12–17 prayerfully, giving special attention to the spiritual virtues Christians should put on.** Once we clear our closets of undesired clothes, we must fill it with the basics we need. When we cleanse our lives of our sinful natures, we put on the attributes of Christ.

A Spiritual Wardrobe

In Colossians 3:12–17, Paul gives some helpful hints about our spiritual wardrobe. As Christian women, we must look our best for Him at every occasion. Paul suggests an eight-piece spiritual wardrobe.

1. *Put on compassion or tender mercies.* In the Old Testament, the Hebrew word *chesed* is translated "mercy" and literally means "unfailing love." God Himself is compassionate and merciful. He desires for His children to care for others too. Mercy is a spiritual gift given by God so that believers will feel genuine empathy and compassion for others. However, all believers must develop mercy and compassion.

   Read Acts 9:36–42. How did Dorcas wear tender mercy?

   _____

   _____

   _____

   _____

2. *Put on kindness.* Kindness has been defined as "steadfast love expressed in actions." God is kind to His children and to all people (Psalm 31:21). He commands His children to be kind to other believers and to other people (Ephesians 4:32). Kindness is a fruit of the Holy Spirit, a virtue to be added to faith.

Read 2 Corinthians 6:3–10. Why must believers wear kindness?

_____

_____

_____

_____

3. *Put on humility.* By nature we are often proud or boastful.
The Bible says that *love "is not conceited"* (1 Corinthians 13:4).
Humility is dependence on God and respect for others.
Believers are to put God and others before self. Humility
gives praise to the power of God not the works of man.

Read Matthew 5:3. What is received by believers who wear humility?

_____

_____

_____

4. *Put on gentleness or meekness.* Weakness and meekness
are not the same. Meekness is a positive quality of gentleness and sensitivity. Submission to God and personal self-
control are reflected through a sweet spirit and pleasant
countenance. Meekness has been described as strength
under control.

Read Matthew 5:5. What is the reward of those who are meek?

_____

_____

_____

5. *Put on patience or longsuffering.* Patience is an attribute of God (Psalm 86:15), a fruit of the Holy Spirit in the believer's life (Galatians 5:22), and an attitude of the heart (1 Corinthians 13:4). It is a difficult virtue to develop. The Greek word translated "patience" literally means "bear up under." Believers need to have patience with God, with self, and with others.

Read James 1:2–4. What can be used to produce patience?

_____

_____

_____

_____

6. *Put on acceptance or tolerance.* Some people and some things are easy to tolerate or put up with; others are not. The Lord endures all things for all times. He calls on His children to wait on Him and to tolerate each other.

Read Proverbs 25:15. What kind of tolerance is often needed to persuade a ruler?

_____

_____

_____

_____

7. *Put on forgiveness.* God's forgiveness is complete, everlasting, and always available. Because God forgives, believers can forgive. Forgiveness is provided by God through an act of obedience. Forgiveness is a personal work by the Holy Spirit and a powerful witness to others.

Read Matthew 6:15. Why is it important for believers to forgive?

_____

_____

_____

_____

8. ***Put on love.*** Loving everybody is not easy. True love is unselfish, loyal, and benevolent concern for others. It is a fruit of the Holy Spirit, the greatest gift of all (1 Corinthians 13:13). Christian love is eternal; it never fails. The Greek word *agape* is an action word meaning "Christlike, selfless love." Above all, the Lord wants us to put on love—*"love covers all offenses"* (Proverbs 10:12).

Read 2 John 5–6. What happens when believers wear love?

_____

_____

_____

_____

_____

_____

These Christian virtues are characteristic of a spiritual wardrobe.

A Protective Wardrobe

In Colossians 3:12–17, Paul speaks of a spiritual wardrobe. He lists the Christian virtues we are to put on. But in another New Testament letter, Paul teaches about a wardrobe for warfare. Christians need to be prepared for the inevitable battle with the evil one, Satan.

Read Ephesians 6:13–18 and in your Bible underline your battle gear.

Dressing protectively for spiritual warfare is important for Christians. Every believer inherits the blessings of God but also the attack of God's enemies. As Satan bombards the believer with temptation, destruction, discouragement, and distraction, Christians must depend on the power of the Holy Spirit for protection. Only then can we withstand evil. In the same way a mother would provide a heavy coat for a child to survive cold temperatures, the Lord provides a protective wardrobe for His children to resist the evil one.

Refer to Ephesians 6:13–18 and describe God's protective wardrobe against spiritual warfare.

Ephesians 6:14 — belt of _____

Ephesians 6:14 — breastplate of _____

Ephesians 6:15 — shoes of the _____

Ephesians 6:16 — shield of _____

Ephesians 6:17 — helmet of _____

Ephesians 6:17 — sword of _____

The Scripture is clear; Christians must put on the full armor of God, not just bits and pieces of battle gear. Wear the belt of *truth*, the breastplate of *righteousness*, shoes of the *gospel*, the shield of *faith*, helmet of *salvation*, and sword of the *Spirit*. Spiritual warfare is serious business and requires complete protection from all sides. The devil is smart and cunning and knows our weaknesses. He will always attack followers of Christ at their point of greatest vulnerability. So, always wear your spiritual protection, and be prepared for personal attacks.

On our seminary campus this semester, it seems we are facing spiritual warfare in greater ways than ever before. Many faculty have parents with serious illnesses; many staff have children with school problems; and many students have critical financial needs. While all of these are common challenges during theological education, they seem more numerous and more intense than in previous years. It should be no surprise to us that the devil is working overtime at New Orleans Baptist Theological Seminary. Our core value focus this year is spiritual vitality. As a seminary, we are reading together through the Bible. With Hurricane Katrina recovery behind us, we are more passionate than ever to reach our city with the gospel. So, of course, the devil is anxious. He is threatened by our living faith, and he is unleashing his demons on us. Spiritual warfare always comes at times of greatest spiritual vitality. Dynamic Christians must wear their warfare wardrobe.

How do we obtain this armor of God? The answer is in Ephesians 6:18: *Pray always!* Prayer is the key to resisting spiritual warfare. Prayer releases God's power to work in our lives, even to defeat the devil. Constant communication with God gives the believer direction and provision. Supplication for others protects them from evil and strengthens the believer who prays from the heart.

What a stunning spiritual wardrobe! If you put on these virtues, you will always be dressed for success. If you wear the armor of God, you will always be protected from spiritual warfare. Now may be the time to inventory your closet, to do some mending, or to give some old clothes away. Let the Lord dress you for His glory!

Prescription 8 for Spiritual Wellness

"Above all, [put on] love — the perfect bond of unity"
(Colossians 3:14).

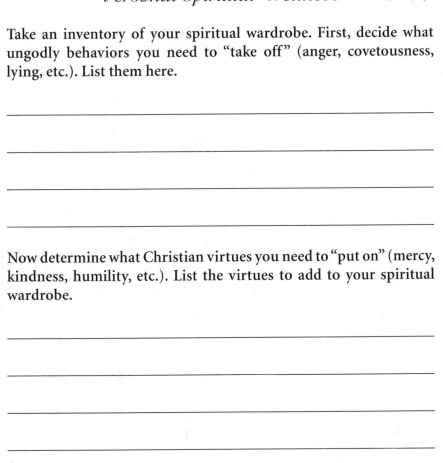

Personal Spiritual Wellness

Take an inventory of your spiritual wardrobe. First, decide what ungodly behaviors you need to "take off" (anger, covetousness, lying, etc.). List them here.

_____

_____

_____

_____

Now determine what Christian virtues you need to "put on" (mercy, kindness, humility, etc.). List the virtues to add to your spiritual wardrobe.

_____

_____

_____

_____

A Submissive Heart

Colossians 3:18–4:1

Introduction

Who has authority in your life? In your family, in your home, in your work, and in your church, there are individuals who have been assigned leadership responsibility in our lives. I have struggled with submission to authority all my life because I am a strong personality. As a young bride, I struggled with submission to my husband until I understood God's design for order in the marriage relationship. Occasionally I struggle with submitting to the spiritual leadership of my pastor or to one of my supervisors at work. You may have struggled with this issue as well. In fact, it is natural for humans to resist the control of others.

For generations, submission has been a perplexing topic of discussion for Christians. Women have struggled to balance the tension between the biblical mandate to submit and the personal desire for independence. Society would have Christian women believe that submission is surrendering self and succumbing to the total control of another. In fact, the human distortion of this biblical teaching at times results in abuse and tyranny. God did not intend for His children to "lord over" each other. Instead, He instituted submission to give order and clear authority to the relationships in life. Authority does not mean superiority; it means ultimate responsibility.

The Greek word *hupotasso*, translated "submissive," literally means "to place under" or "to line up under." In His divine wisdom, God knew that authority must be established for human relationships to function effectively. So, He gave clear instructions about how to relate to each other. God desires first for His children to submit willingly to Him—to give Him total control of life. Then

He commands us to be submissive to others who have been placed in authority over us.

Read the following Scriptures that teach about biblical submission. Think carefully about how each teaching affects your life.

1. Hebrews 12:9—Submit first to God.

2. Romans 13:1–2—All authority is ordained by God.

3. 1 Peter 3:1–2—Choose to submit. Submission is an act of the will.

4. Ephesians 5:21–24—Submission pleases God.

5. Ephesians 5:25—Submission is a response to love.

Now write your own definition of biblical submission.

_____

_____

_____

_____

_____

_____

The Bible teaches all believers to totally surrender to the Lord and willingly submit to others in authority. Carefully read Colossians 3:18–4:1, then fill in the blanks below.

Wives, be submissive to _____(v. 18).

Husbands, love _____(v. 19).

Children, obey _____(v. 20).

Fathers, do not exasperate _____(v. 21).

Slaves, obey _____(v. 22).

Masters, supply your slaves _____(v. 4:1).

Now let's examine God's plan for these human relationships.

Wives and Husbands

Throughout Scripture, God uses the marriage relationship to teach important truths. He taught about His role in the church by using a marital analogy. The church is called the *bride of Christ* (2 Corinthians 11:2). Therefore, Christ is understood to be the bridegroom of the church, the head of the body of Christ, the one in authority over all believers.

Scripture assigns a specific role to the husband and the wife in marriage. Different roles do not affect the worth of an individual. God created male and female in His own image, equal in worth and value, but different in role and function (Genesis 1:27). These roles help maintain order and establish authority in marriage. The Bible teaches that submission is an important part of marriage.

Reread these three passages to understand better biblical submission: Ephesians 5:21–22; Colossians 3:18; and 1 Peter 3:1.

Now list several biblical principles about submission in marriage.

_____

_____

_____

_____

While voluntary surrendering of self is difficult, it is God's plan. Wives are to submit to their husbands as they submit to God (Ephesians 5:22). Submission of the wife to her husband is God's perfect plan for marriage (Colossians 3:18). And, the wife's willing submission to her husband can be a powerful witness in the world (1 Peter 3:1). Understanding submission is a great challenge, but an even greater challenge is for a couple to demonstrate a submissive spirit every day.

Consider the following ways wives are to submit to their husbands. The Amplified translation of Ephesians 5:33 says, *"Let the wife see that she respects and reverences her husband, [that she notices him, honors him, prefers him, venerates and esteems him, and that she defers to him, praises him, regards him, and loves and admires him exceedingly]"* (AMP). This Scripture paraphrase cites ten specific ways for wives to show submission to their husbands.

1. *Notice him.* Wives should pay attention to their husbands and not ignore them.

2. *Regard him.* Women should affirm their husbands and the efforts their husbands make to lead the family.

3. *Honor him.* Wives should respect their husbands, not put them down or belittle them.

4. *Prefer him.* Wives should desire to be with their husbands, enjoying them and enjoying spending time together.

5. *Venerate him.* Wives should admire and defer to their husbands.

6. *Esteem him.* Wives should value and treasure their husbands.

7. *Defer to him.* Wives should support the decisions of their husbands.

8. *Praise him.* Wives should affirm and encourage their husbands. Affirmation is a basic need of most men.

9. *Love him.* Wives should care deeply for their husbands, expressing affection and care.

10. *Admire him.* Wives should be devoted to their husbands, acknowledging their strengths.

While submission seems to be an overwhelming responsibility for the wife, husbands are to love their wives as much as Christ loves the church (Ephesians 5:25–27). Paul used five verbs to describe Christ's relationship to His bride — the church. He loved her, gave Himself for her, made her holy, cleansed her, and presented her to Himself. Christ expressed sacrificial love to His bride so that she could be complete. A husband is to love his wife sacrificially and strengthen her through the bonds of marriage.

In Colossians 3:19, Paul warns husbands not to be bitter toward their wives. This warning about bitterness is not recorded in any other Scripture referring to the role of husbands. **Why do you think Paul voiced this concern at this time?**

_____

_____

_____

_____

_____

_____

Biblical love is expressed in both words and actions. Husbands must be careful to state their love and live it out. A wife often measures a husband's love by the way he treats her. If she does not consistently experience love, she can develop bitterness.

In addition, a husband can become bitter toward his wife if he is resentful about his responsibilities or disappointed in her. Paul reminds husbands to love their wives and not treat them harshly.

Children and Parents

Jesus modeled biblical submission for us. He submitted Himself completely to God (Luke 22:41–3). He was submissive to governmental authorities (Luke 22:47–54), and He was submissive to others in positions of authority (John 13:1–7). Jesus Christ was also submissive to His earthly parents, Joseph and Mary (Luke 2:46–52). The Bible assigns parents and children a reciprocal responsibility. While children are to obey their parents, parents are not to provoke or exasperate their children. As the authorities in the home, parents are to love their children, and children are to respond in obedience.

All children are to obey their parents. The Greek word for "children" (*tekna*) is a general term, not limited to a specific age group. The Greek word for "obey" (*hupakouete*) means continually obeying. In other words, children should continue always to obey their parents from the time they are young and throughout adulthood. Why? Paul stated the motive for obedience. It is *"pleasing in the Lord"* (Colossians 3:20). Love and obedience are lifelong behaviors in the parent-child relationship.

As children grow up, they may have different opinions from their parents. They may resist adult guidance and rebel against parental authority. However, Christians who submit their lives to the Lord should willingly obey their parents because of God's instruction. Throughout life, strong individuals must yield their own ways for God's way. As in marriage, this reciprocal relationship between parent and child is more natural when each is following God's divine plan.

In Ephesians 6:4 and Colossians 3:21, fathers are addressed directly. Previously, both parents are mentioned, but now Paul focuses on the father. Typically, the mother is the nurturer in the home and the father is the disciplinarian. Paul warns fathers not to provoke or irritate their children, as they might become discouraged or disheartened. Instead, fathers are to train their children in the Lord.

Can you think of some ways that fathers can exasperate their children? List them here.

_____

_____

_____

_____

_____

_____

Children could be easily exasperated by the harshness or strictness of a father. However, they can be encouraged and strengthened by their fathers' love. Fathers need to give their children four A's:

Acceptance: self-worth and security

Appreciation: affirmation and praise

Affection: love and care

Availability: time and attention

The pattern of love and obedience in the parent-child relationship was first given by the Lord in the Ten Commandments. In Exodus 20:12, children are instructed to *"honor your father and your mother so that you may have a long life in the land that the LORD your God is giving you."* Then in Exodus 21:17 the consequence of disobedience to parents are given: *"Whoever curses his father or his mother must be put to death."* God's law commands that all children respect and obey their parents at all times or suffer the consequences of God's judgment. Parents who raise their children in the love of God should receive the utmost appreciation and obedience from their children.

Employees and Employers

Paul addressed the roles of three different human relationships in Colossians 3:18–4:1. These Scriptures clearly state how people should respond to those in authority—wives to husbands, children to parents, and slaves to masters. Obedience and submission are a part of God's plan.

First, Paul told them how. Obedience is to come from the heart. Simple compliance in actions is not enough. Employees are to follow willingly their employers—because of reverence for God. Second, he told employees to work hard. Diligent work is a service to God. In 1 Peter 2:18, employees are instructed to obey all managers, even the harsh or difficult ones. Finally, Paul reminds workers of the rewards of obedience. Though obedience is often difficult, in His time God blesses those who obey Him.

Many people today are in the workplace. For Christian women working outside the home, the workplace becomes a missions field. Godly behavior plus a verbal witness can lead co-workers to the Lord. God's plan for workers to obey their bosses not only gives order in the office, but the righteous relationship can be a witness in the world. When you respect and follow the leadership of your employer with a willing and cooperative spirit, your life testifies of your submission to the Lord and your obedience to His will.

Read the following Scriptures and identify some rewards of submission. Record in the space provided a blessing that comes to believers who follow God's plan for human relationships.

1. 1 Peter 3:1 _____

2. 1 Peter 3:5–6 _____

3. Ephesians 5:32–33 _____

4. Titus 2:3–5 _____

5. 1 Peter 3:4 _____

6. 1 Peter 3:7 _____

Submission should be the natural result of a deep love for the Lord. Though there should be no desire for personal gain, the Bible promises blessings to believers who obey His teachings. Unbelieving husbands can be won to the Lord by the witness of a submissive wife (1 Peter 3:1). Submissive women are called holy like Sarah, Rebekah, Rachel, and Leah (1 Peter 3:5–6). A submissive wife will be loved by her husband as much as he loves himself (Ephesians 5:32–33). A submissive wife can teach younger women how to love their own husbands and submit to his loving leadership (Titus 2:3–5). A submissive woman develops a godly spirit, which is gentle and quiet (1 Peter 3:4). And, submissive women will be loved and protected by their husbands (1 Peter 3:7). What great rewards for obedience!

Ultimately, the greatest reward for obedience is received by the believer in heaven. People may not always appreciate their efforts, but God will offer eternal rewards to those who follow His pattern for human relationships. What a relief to know that we don't have to please others; we must please God.

Prescription 9 for Spiritual Wellness

"Whatever you do, do it enthusiastically, as something done for the Lord and not for men" (Colossians 3:23).

Personal Spiritual Wellness

Periodically every Christian needs to examine her heart, especially her attitude about submitting to the authority of others.

How submissive are you to God, your husband (if married), your father (if unmarried), your employer, spiritual leaders, and government officials? Identify three ways you can practice healthy submission to those in authority over you. Write your plans below.

1. _____

_____

_____

2. _____

_____

_____

3. _____

_____

_____

Lesson 10
The Speech of a Believer
Colossians 4:2–6

Introduction

The Apostle Paul made a significant contribution to Christianity through his missionary journeys and New Testament epistles. He preached, taught, and wrote about some of the most important doctrines of the faith. But, do you know what Paul wrote most about? He wrote about behavior. More than anything else, Paul challenged Christians to live godly lives. He believed Christians should act differently than non-Christians—that believers actually became like new persons after conversion.

Behavior is the way a person conducts herself. The actions of a person reflect outwardly whom the person is inside. Thus Paul exhorted Christians to live the life of Christ in the world. In the Book of Colossians, Paul first addressed the personal behavior of the believer (Colossians 3:5–17). Then he discussed the behavior of Christians at home (Colossians 3:18–4:1). In Colossians 4:2–6, he described the verbal behavior of the believer. Even the speech of a believer should be unlike the unbeliever, like Christ spoke while He lived on earth.

Reflect for a moment on Paul's many teachings about behavior.

Romans 12:9–21	*Christian Behavior*
1 Corinthians 13:1–13	*Loving Behavior*
2 Corinthians 7:2–12	*Repentant Behavior*
Galatians 5:22–23	*Fruitful Behavior*

Ephesians 5:22–6:4	*Family Behavior*
Philippians 2:1–11	*Humble Behavior*
Colossians 2:6–10	*Faithful Behavior*
1 Thessalonians 2:1–12	*Paul's Own Behavior*
2 Thessalonians 3:6–15	*Hard Working Behavior*
1 Timothy 3:1–3	*Behavior of Church Leaders*
2 Timothy 1:7–12	*Bold Behavior*
Titus 2:1–8	*Mentoring Behavior*
Philemon 17–22	*Obedient Behavior*

Paul was thorough in his biblical discussion of Christian behavior. He wisely included speech as a behavior for Christians to improve. In several of his letters, Paul discussed the characteristics of godly speech.

Read these verses and write a teaching about the believer's speech.

1 Corinthians 2:6–7 _____

_____

_____

2 Corinthians 12:6–7 _____

_____

_____

Ephesians 4:15 _____

_____

_____

Ephesians 4:32 _____

_____

_____

Colossians 4:6 _____

_____

_____

Titus 2:15 _____

_____

_____

The Christian's speech should contain the wisdom of God not only the knowledge of man (1 Corinthians 2:6–7). Christians should speak the truth of God and give glory to Him (2 Corinthians 12:6–7). And, the truth spoken by Christians should be offered in love, kindness, compassion, and forgiveness just as Christ (Ephesians 4:15, 32). The speech of a believer should be gracious responses in love (Colossians 4:6). And, a Christian's words should encourage others and rebuke or correct when necessary, all in a spirit of God's love (Titus 2:15).

Speech is a behavior; thankfully, for Christians, a learned behavior. Therefore, it is a behavior that we can change. God calls us to have the speech of a believer. In Colossians 4:2–6, speech is discussed on three levels. **Read these verses carefully to understand how Christians are to speak _to_ God, speak _of_ Him, and speak _like_ Him.**

Speak to God

Paul talked often about the importance of prayer—communication with God. At the very beginning of the Book of Colossians, he gave specific ways to pray—lift up others, thank the Father, and ask for power (Colossians 1:3–12). He teaches us to pray by example and by instruction in the same way that Jesus did in Matthew 6:5–15.

As Paul moves to the close of his letter to the Christians in Colossae, he reminds them again of the importance of prayer. Twice in Colossians 4:2 he expresses the urgency of prayer when he says *"devote yourselves to prayer"* and *"stay alert."* The believer is to be fervent in prayer—speaking to God continually, faithfully, and passionately.

Read this translation of the same verse: *"Devote yourselves to prayer, keeping alert in it with an attitude of thanksgiving"* **(Colossians 4:2 NASB). Now write this verse in your own words.**

_____

_____

_____

_____

_____

_____

Christians are to have active prayer lives, devoting themselves to prayer. The Greek word *proskartere* is translated "devote yourselves" and means "to be steadfast" or "to endure." So an active prayer life is constant, ongoing, continual. Active prayer is alert—always noticing the needs of others. Christians are to be watchful, alert to the needs of the world and the will of God. In a practical way, believers need to find their ideal time to pray when they are alert and fresh.

For many years I struggled with the verse that says, *"O God, You are my God, early will I seek you"* (Psalm 63:1 NKJV). You see, I'm not a morning person! My husband teases that I don't believe in God until 10:00 A.M. I always respond that I believe in God before 10:00 A.M., I just don't act like it. You can imagine my joy when I discovered the Holman Christian Standard Bible translation of that same verse: *"I eagerly seek You"* (Psalm 63:1). I do want to seek the Lord, but I need to be alert. Early mornings are not best for me. Believers need to find their best time to pray. *That* you pray is more important than *when* you pray.

Finally, Paul says prayer requires an attitude of thanksgiving. Throughout the Book of Colossians, the apostle has stressed the importance of a grateful heart. Be grateful for salvation (1:12). Be grateful for spiritual growth (2:6). Be grateful for fellowship with Christ and His church (3:15). Be grateful for the opportunity to serve (3:17). And be grateful that God answers prayer (4:2–4). These are five excellent "Be Attitudes" about prayer.

My sweet mother-in-love is a woman of prayer. She follows this biblical mandate to be devoted to prayer. She rises early every morning to spend several hours in prayer for family and friends. She remains alert to the needs of others and updates her prayer lists regularly. Mom Kelley also expresses thanksgiving in everything. Throughout the day, you hear her utter from her heart the words *thank you, God*. She is mindful that everything good is from the Lord. What an important reminder to all of us to be devoted to prayer and diligent to thank the Lord for all things!

Speak of Him

In verses 3 and 4, Paul encourages believers to pray for him and for the others who ministered with him. *Us* in Colossians 4:3 probably refers to Timothy and all Christians in Rome plus the apostle Paul himself. He specifically requested prayer for them as they witnessed. Open doors (opportunities) and a clear word (testimony) are necessary witnessing tools. Prayer is the key that unlocks the door of an unbeliever's heart to the witness of a Christian. Pray that you will speak of Him boldly! Pray for other Christians to be bold witnesses.

While lifestyle evangelism is effective in opening doors to the lost, a verbal witness is essential for the spread of the gospel. Paul not only desired prayer for opportunities, but specifically for opportunities for ministry, *"to speak the mystery of the Messiah"* (Colossians 4:3).

Reread Colossians 1:26–27, which addresses the "mystery" of the Old Testament revealed in the New Testament. That mystery that needs to be shared verbally is the gospel — *"Christ in you, the hope of glory."*

In Colossians 4:6, Paul encourages believers to season their speech with salt. What does that command mean to you?

_____

_____

_____

_____

The words of a Christian should be seasoned with the grace of God and well chosen to encourage others. Salt preserves, purifies, and flavors. The speech of a Christian should have that same effect on the unsaved. Jesus Christ shared His living water with the woman at the well who was spiritually thirsty. He said to her, *"whoever drinks from the water that I will give him will never get thirsty again — ever"* (John 4:14). The loving words of a Christian can lead to witness.

I have been reminded several times recently that kind words are powerful. When you greet people with a joyful hello, they stop and give you attention. When you respond to a question with a positive, upbeat answer, people listen. When your voice lifts up and your words encourage, listeners are impacted by your speech.

During a recent trip to the drugstore, I called Mom Kelley to see if she needed anything from the store. Apparently, my kind voice and loving words were overheard by other people. A store manager told me that was the nicest phone call he had ever heard and asked me to call his mother to be nice to her. Upon leaving the store, another shopper asked me to make nice phone calls at the drugstore every Monday morning to remind her to be nice. I could share with both of them that I could be nice because of God's love in me. Speak of God!

Paul's final phrase in Colossians 4:6 reminds believers of the importance of a personal witness. Each believer must be sensitive to the needs of others and depend on the Holy Spirit's guidance to say just the right thing. Fear is the most common obstacle to witnessing. Christians fear inadequacy, rejection, and failure as they speak of Him. In another epistle, Paul reminds us that *"God has not given us a spirit of fearfulness, but one of power, love, and sound judgment"* (2 Timothy 1:7). Remember that the power of the Holy Spirit is with you as you speak the gospel.

Speak Like Him

Do you agree with this age-old proverb: actions speak louder than words? Whether you want to believe it or not, it is true. Your actions overshadow your words. What you do is heard louder than what you say. For the Christian, both the verbal witness and a lifestyle of godliness are necessary if others are to receive the gospel message. If a Christian does not live like Christ, a word of witness will not be effective.

Colossians 4:5 says, *"Walk in wisdom toward outsiders."* In other words, behave with wisdom toward unbelievers (see also 1 Corinthians 5:12–13; 1 Thessalonians 4:12; 1 Timothy 3:7). Let's examine the word *wisdom* to know how to act. *Wisdom* means "the ability to collect and concisely organize principles from Scripture." The Christian is to live out biblical principles.

In the Book of 1 Corinthians, Paul contrasted worldly wisdom and scriptural wisdom.

Read 1 Corinthians 3:18–4:5 then list several characteristics of wisdom.

Worldly Wisdom	Spiritual Wisdom
1. _____	1. _____
2. _____	2. _____

3. _____   3. _____
4. _____   4. _____
5. _____   5. _____

In this passage, Paul the Apostle describes worldly or human wisdom as foolish. In other words, human wisdom is limited, faulty, and even ridiculous. On the other hand, spiritual wisdom is from God; God alone knows everything, even what is a mystery to us. God alone will judge or evaluate us because He alone is omniscient. Ask God to give you spiritual wisdom that is reflected in your speech and actions.

Speech is a difficult behavior to control. But God can give us the power to speak to Him, speak of Him, and speak like Him. The behavior of a believer should be Christlike and Christ-pleasing. Psalm 19:14 challenges all believers to discipline their words and thoughts.

Write your name in the blanks below to personalize the pronoun *my*. Then pray this prayer to God from Psalm 19:14.

Let the words of _____ 's mouth
And the meditation of _____'s heart
Be acceptable in Your sight,
O Lord, _____'s strength
and _____'s Redeemer.

Prescription 10 for Spiritual Wellness

"Your speech should always be gracious, seasoned with salt, so that you may know how you should answer each person" (Colossians 4:6).

Personal Spiritual Wellness

If actions speak louder than words, perhaps you should carefully examine your actions. Do your actions speak of God and His great love?

Think of three things you have done recently that spoke of God to others. Record them below.

1. _____

2. _____

3. _____

Commit your actions to Him each day.

A Fond Farewell
Colossians 4:7–18

Introduction

The time had come for Paul to bid a fond farewell to the church at Colossae, to Christian friends he had never met. Though he had not visited the Colossians, Paul felt a close kinship with the fellow believers because of his faithful prayers for them. He challenged them to continue in their faith (Colossians 4:2–6) and then began his lingering good-bye (Colossians 4:7–18). Saying good-bye to ones you love is often hard, especially if you have an important message to communicate.

I always have a hard time saying good-bye to my sister, Mitzi. When we talk on the telephone, our conversation can go on for hours, and we frequently say good-bye a dozen times before we hang up. We always think of one more thing to say, one more question to ask, one more message to pass along. So, our good-byes can go on for some time. I understand Paul's hesitation to end his letter. He thought of one more thing to say, one more question to ask, one more message to pass along. But in Colossians 4:18 he finally said *amen*, good-bye, the end.

Paul struggled with good-byes in all his New Testament letters. He loved his friends in the ministry and always greeted them fondly. In the Book of Romans, he greeted several co-laborers in the faith, and then gave God the glory forever (Romans 16:19–27). In 1 and 2 Corinthians, Paul exhorted several servants of Christ and extended grace and love (1 Corinthians 16:13–24 and 2 Corinthians 13:11–13). In Galatians, Ephesians, and Philippians, he encouraged believers and offered God's grace, peace, and love to them (Galatians 6:11–18; Ephesians 6:21–24; Philippians 4:21–23). In 1 and 2 Thessalonians and 1 and 2 Timothy, Titus, and Philemon, Paul blesses his friends in the faith before giving greetings of peace and grace (1 Thessalonians 5:12–28; 2 Thessalonians 3:16–18; 1 Timothy 6:20–21; 2 Timothy 4:9–22; Titus 3:12–15; Philemon 23–25). Paul's fond farewells gave God glory and portrayed a positive impression of the apostle.

In his opening greeting in Colossians, Paul identified himself and his intended audience (Colossians 1:1–2). Then he extended grace and peace to them from God the Father and the Lord Jesus Christ. As he concluded his letter, Paul identified those companions who had labored for Christ with him (Colossians 4:7–14), and he acknowledged more specifically the recipients of his letter (Colossians 4:15).

Take time now to read Colossians 4:7–18. List below those co-workers Paul identified.

1. _____

2. _____

3. _____

4. _____

5. _____

6. _____

7. _____

8. _____

9. _____

10. _____

Paul gave a brief personal introduction of these co-laborers in the Book of Colossians; then he expressed closing greetings and a final blessing. This format is similar to other epistles, a typical

Greco-Roman correspondence form with the greeting at the end. However, his style and expression vary somewhat from his other writings. Biblical experts agree that Paul probably wrote this letter about the same time he wrote Philemon (A.D. 60–63). The account of Paul's imprisonment in Rome and the setting of his writings are recorded in Acts 28:30–31. Now let's carefully examine the last few verses of Colossians.

Personal Introductions

In Colossians 4:7–18, Paul the apostle identified by name ten different believers who ministered with him. Look back at your previous assignment to see if you correctly listed all ten individuals. How did you do? Next, we will learn more about these faithful Christians who were acknowledged by Paul in this letter.

Tychicus [TIK-ih-kuhs]
Paul immediately identified a trusted friend and companion, Tychicus.

Read the following passages, then write what you learn about this man of God: Acts 20:1–4; Ephesians 6:21; Colossians 4:7–9; 2 Timothy 4:12; and Titus 3:12.

_____

_____

_____

_____

Tychicus means "fortunate." Indeed, Tychicus was fortunate to serve and minister with Paul. But the apostle was also blessed to have a faithful co-worker. Paul's love for Tychicus was obvious, and Tychicus's devotion to Paul and the Lord were evidenced in his actions. He delivered the letter and important information to the Christians in Colossae. He was greatly used by God in building the early church.

Onesimus [oh-NESS-ih-muhs]
In contrast to the character of Tychicus, Paul mentions another companion, Onesimus, a runaway slave.

Read Colossians 4:9 and Philemon 10–16 before you write a brief description of this Christian friend.

_____

_____

_____

_____

Onesimus was apparently the slave of Philemon, a leader in the Colossian church. He ran away to Rome, where Onesimus was led to Christ by Paul. He accompanied Tychicus with the letter from Paul to Colossae. Paul pleaded with Philemon to forgive Onesimus and welcome him back as a new man in Christ.

Aristarchus [ehr-iss-TAHR-kuhs]
Little is known from Scripture about Aristarchus. Read these passages in Acts (19:29; 20:4; 27:2) in addition to Colossians 4:10.

What did you learn about Aristarchus?

_____

_____

_____

_____

Aristarchus was a Jewish believer from the city of Thessalonica in the region of Macedonia. He was imprisoned in Rome with Paul at the time of this writing. The accounts in the Book of Acts record the supportive role Aristarchus played in Paul's ministry. He was a dependable co-laborer, always present when Paul needed him—facing an angry mob (Acts 19:29), returning to Jerusalem (Acts 20:4), or traveling to Rome (Acts 27:4). The ministry of Paul the Apostle was strengthened by the faithful efforts of believers like Aristarchus.

Mark (also called John Mark)
John Mark was with Paul again in Rome. He is truly a complex individual who had returned to minister with Paul.

Read these selected passages and write about this man of renewed faith: 2 Timothy 4:11; Philemon 23–24; 1 Peter 5:13.

_____

_____

_____

_____

The cousin of Barnabas, Mark ministered not only with Paul but with Peter and Timothy as well. Mark accompanied Paul and Barnabas on the first missionary journey (Acts 12:25–14:28). However, John Mark left them abruptly and returned to Jerusalem (Acts 13:13). Paul was disappointed with Mark's lack of commitment and later disagreed with Barnabas about his participation in the third missionary journey (Acts 15:36–40). Details about the separation are unclear, but Mark returned to serve with Paul. While he didn't actually minister with Jesus, he witnessed much of the work of the early church. He wrote one of the four Gospels recording the life and work of Jesus Christ.

Justus [JUHS-tuhs]
Only one verse in Scripture mentions *"Jesus who is called Justus"* (Colossians 4:11). He is included in Paul's discussion of Jewish believers who are *"alone of the circumcision"* (Colossians 4:11)—Tychicus, Onesimus, Aristarchus, Mark, and Justus.

Next Paul mentions other Christian workers.

Epaphras [EP-uh-frass]
Epaphras is the only person mentioned earlier in the Book of Colossians.

Read Colossians 1:7 and 4:12–13, and then describe this fellow bondservant.

_____

_____

_____

Converted during Paul's ministry in Ephesus, Epaphras is apparently the pastor of the Colossian church who is visiting with Paul in Rome. He was instrumental in spreading the gospel to the Lychus Valley and served as a messenger between Paul and the Christians in Colossae. Paul recognized him as a committed prayer warrior. He was a real-life example of one who continually and vigilantly prayed (Colossians 4:2).

Luke
The beloved physician and another writer of the Gospels, Luke was with Paul in Rome.

What a host of characters accompanied Paul during his ministry! Read these verses and write a brief description of this familiar man named Luke: Colossians 4:14; 2 Timothy 4:11; Philemon 24.

_____

_____

_____

_____

Luke was apparently Paul's personal physician and close friend. He frequently traveled with Paul and remained with him as his ministry drew to a close. At times, only Luke was with Paul (2 Timothy 4:11). While little more background is known about Luke, he obviously enjoyed a special relationship with the great apostle.

Demas [DEE-muhs]

Though his name is unfamiliar to many Christians today, Demas was identified by Paul in three of his letters.

Read the following references: Colossians 4:14; 2 Timothy 4:10; Philemon 24. What does the Bible say about Demas?

_____

_____

_____

_____

Demas is included in the list of co-laborers with Paul. However, Paul stops short of offering praise for Demas. In 2 Timothy 4:10, Paul reports that he left his faith: Demas _"loved this present world."_ How sad for a child of God to turn to sin! Paul must have had a broken heart. Ministers today are heartbroken when Christians leave the Lord. Pray for those who have left their first love.

Nympha [NIM-fuh]

Read Colossians 4:15 and record what you learn about this believer.

_____

_____

_____

In Colossians 4:15 Paul asks the Colossians to greet other believ-ers—those in Laodicea, Nympha, and members of her church. Some biblical scholars do not isolate Nympha as an individual named by Paul as a co-laborer. Other translators identify Nympha as a female (see Colossians 4:15). What Scripture does say is that a church or body of believers was meeting together in Nympha's home. All New Testament churches met in homes (for example, Acts 12:12; Romans 16:5; 1 Corinthians 16:19; Philemon 2). Paul sent greetings to Nympha and the church members there.

Archippus [AHR-kip-uhs]
At the end of this letter, Paul mentions a final Christian brother, Archippus. His name appears only in Colossians 4:17 and Philemon 2.

What do these verses tell you about Archippus?

_____

_____

_____

_____

_____

Archippus undoubtedly was a faithful believer, a fellow soldier in the spread of the gospel. He was an active member of the church that met in Philemon's home (Philemon 2). Archippus may have been the son of Philemon and Apphia. The verse in Colossians (v. 17) records Paul's exhortation to young Archippus to remain faithful to his call to ministry. Because of the disobedience of Demas, Paul reminded Archippus and all Christians of the need for persistent obedience.

If you were writing a letter to Christian friends, who would you introduce to them, and how would you describe your colleagues in the ministry? God's work is being accomplished by a multitude of His followers. It is important to acknowledge the many who serve the Lord faithfully. Paul's recognition of his co-laborers was a tribute to them and an example for us. All who serve the Lord faithfully are to be praised in a way that gives God the glory.

Closing Greetings

In the final section of Colossians, Paul identifies Christian companions and co-laborers. Then, he expresses his closing greetings. Initially Paul sends greetings from those ministering with him.

- Aristarchus, with Mark and Justus (Colossians 4:10)
- Epaphras (Colossians 4:12)
- Luke and Demas (Colossians 4:14)

Then Paul asks the Colossians to greet specific individuals (see Colossians 4:15).

- brethren in Laodicea
- Nympha
- the members of the church at Nympha's house.

What do you think is the purpose of the greeting in a New Testament letter?

_____

_____

_____

_____

Did Paul accomplish the purpose in his epistle to the Colossians?

_____

_____

Explain.

_____

_____

_____

_____

What is an epistle?

_____

_____

_____

_____

_____

In a recent cartoon strip, an epistle was defined as "the New Testament version of email." Certainly, the word _epistle_ is not used very often in daily conversation today. But, Christians should be familiar with this biblical term.

An epistle is an instructive letter. The Bible includes many letters—some are mentioned in Bible books, while others are the entire book of the Bible. More than half of the New Testament books are epistles. The apostle Paul wrote 13 of the New Testament letters, which are often referred to as Pauline Epistles.

In another comic strip, a young boy asks his Sunday School teacher, "How did Paul send his letters—by regular mail, Fed Ex, or email?" Obviously Paul's letters were delivered personally by Christian friends. Sending letters was the primary form of communication for the early church. And, Paul's message was delivered during this life and throughout time.

Final Blessing

The personal introductions and closing greeting are followed by Paul's final blessing. Before you read Colossians 4:18, reread Colossians 1:2. Paul opens and closes this letter to the Colossian Christians the same way. He extends to them *"grace"* from God.

Paul's final blessing was the same in all of his epistles. Read each biblical reference below, then fill in the blank to complete Paul's blessing to his Christian friends.

Romans 16:24 — *"The _____ of our Lord Jesus Christ be with you all."*

1 Corinthians 16:23–24 — *"The _____ of our Lord Jesus Christ be with you. My _____ be with all of you in Christ Jesus."*

2 Corinthians 13:13 — *"The _____ of the Lord Jesus Christ, and the _____ of God, and the _____ of the Holy Spirit be with all of you."*

Galatians 6:18 — *"Brothers, the _____ of our Lord Jesus Christ be with your spirit."*

Ephesians 6:24 — *"_____ be with all who have undying love for our Lord Jesus Christ."*

Philippians 4:23 — *"The _____ of our Lord Jesus Christ be with your spirit."*

Colossians 4:18 — *"_____ be with you."*

1 Thessalonians 5:28 — *"May the _____ of our Lord*

Jesus Christ be with you!"

2 Thessalonians 3:18 — *"The _____ of our Lord Jesus*

Christ be with all of you."

1 Timothy 6:21 — *"_____ be with all of you."*

2 Timothy 4:22 — *"_____ be with you!"*

Titus 3:15 — *"_____ be with all of you."*

Philemon 25 — *"The _____ of the Lord Jesus Christ be with*

your spirit."

While Paul occasionally added to his final blessing, he always extended grace to those Christians who received his letter.

Why do you think *"grace"* was always the last word uttered by Paul?

Salvation by grace through faith was the primary message of Paul's ministry and writings. Once and for all, he wanted Christians to understand that salvation was by faith and not works. It is the gracious gift of the Lord Jesus Christ. Paul had found God's grace to be sufficient for all his needs. He frequently emphasized in his closings that grace was for *"all."* He dispelled the belief that only the Jewish people were chosen for salvation. God's grace is for all — the Jew and the Greek, male and female. What an amazing grace gift from God!

Prescription 11 for Wellness

"Pay attention to the ministry you have received in the Lord, so that you can accomplish it" (Colossians 4:17).

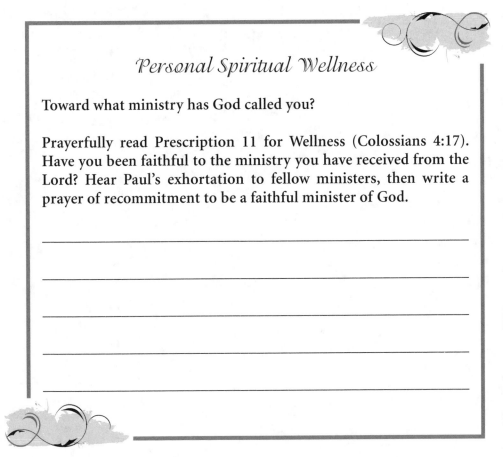

Personal Spiritual Wellness

Toward what ministry has God called you?

Prayerfully read Prescription 11 for Wellness (Colossians 4:17). Have you been faithful to the ministry you have received from the Lord? Hear Paul's exhortation to fellow ministers, then write a prayer of recommitment to be a faithful minister of God.

_____

_____

_____

_____

_____

Faith and Fitness
Conclusion

Introduction

You have now completed this study of the Book of Colossians written by the apostle Paul. You have considered many different topics. You have discovered many biblical truths. You have concentrated on several doctrines. But overall, you have focused on faith and fitness. Now you may be better able to answer the question, *How can Christians stay spiritually fit?* The Book of Colossians is truly "A Woman's Guide to Spiritual Wellness."

Many Christians place themselves at risk spiritually when they don't strengthen their faith. A weak Christian is vulnerable to spiritual illness in the same way that a frail person is susceptible to physical illness. For years, the medical field was focused on sickness—eliminating or treating disease. But now, doctors are most concerned about the total wellness of their patients. They emphasize preventive medicine and healthy lifestyles. Wellness is "a dynamic process of improving one's health status at any phase or in any dimension of health." Wellness affects the whole person.

The Bible advocates spiritual wellness. Christians should not wait for spiritual illness to occur, and then treat it. Instead, growing Christians must work to prevent spiritual decline and alter their lifestyles to promote total wellness. Paul discussed well being in 1 Thessalonians 5:23:

> *"Now may the God of peace Himself sanctify you entirely [or wholly]; and may your spirit and soul and body be preserved complete, without blame at the coming of our Lord Jesus Christ"* (NASB).

God desires His children to be wholly holy until He comes again.

Conclusion

In the Book of Colossians, Paul taught many biblical truths that you can practice to develop your spiritual wellness.

Reflect on these basic teachings that should influence a believer's daily life.

Prayer Pleases God	Colossians 1:1–12
Christ Is God Incarnate, the Only Way to Salvation	Colossians 1:13–23
Christians Should Rejoice in Suffering	Colossians 1:24–29
Believers Are Built Up in Christ	Colossians 2:1–15
Christians Should Add Nothing to Faith	Colossians 2:16–23
The Christian Life Is Set Apart	Colossians 3:1–11
Christians Must Put on Love	Colossians 3:12–17
Christians Must Be Submissive as Unto the Lord	Colossians 3:18–4:1
Believers Must Speak Like Christ	Colossians 4:2–6

Tommy Yessick, a wellness expert and author of *Building Blocks for Longer Life and Ministry,* suggests that there are six dimensions of wellness: emotional, intellectual, occupational, physical, social, and spiritual. Let's review Colossians to see what the apostle Paul had to say about each dimension of wellness. As you read each passage, be sure to examine your own personal health. A Christian cannot be spiritually well unless she is healthy emotionally, intellectually, occupationally, physically, and socially, as well as spiritually.

Emotional Well-Being

Emotional well-being is perceived by mental health professionals to be the stabilizing factor for all the other wellness dimensions. God created humans as emotional beings, with feelings and attitudes. He desires for His children to have a passion for Him and deep feelings for others. Emotions are a person's way to express the feelings within. Women are especially emotional creatures. The experiences of life bring pain or joy, sadness or anger for a woman. Healthy emotional wellbeing bonds believers to God and to each other in deep relationships.

Paul freely expressed his emotions in his letters to Christians of the early church. He voiced feelings of love, concern, and understanding. In Colossians 2:1–3, Paul's passionate feelings for the Christians in Colossae were obvious. **Read that passage of Scripture, then list some of the emotions experienced by Paul.**

_____

_____

_____

_____

The deep feelings of Paul toward friends in the faith were clearly visible.

- *"How great a struggle I have for you"*

- *"I want their hearts to be encouraged"*

- *"Joined together in love"*

I am a very emotional person. In fact, I cry often, whether I am happy or sad, refreshed or fatigued, agreeable or angry. I have often asked the Lord to dry up my tears. But, He always reminds me of His tender heart. I do want to have a heart like His — a heart of compassion and care and concern. A tender heart is a tearful heart. So, get out the tissues, friends. Now I just ask the Lord to help me control my tears so that my words of witness can be understood clearly.

It is essential for Christians to be well *emotionally* and healthy in all areas of their lives. Now let's examine intellectual well-being.

Intellectual Well-Being

Intellectual or mental well-being is the human's ability to think, to learn, and to explore and understand information. The human mind is an amazing creation of God. With our minds, we can reason, have opinions, acquire knowledge, increase awareness, and sharpen perception. It is important, however, for Christians to guard their minds from evil and use their mental powers for good. Intellectual well-being requires the believer to be alert, rational, and sensible.

In Colossians 2:8–10, Paul warns the Colossians to protect their minds from false teachings. Many Christians were believing and following the principles of the world. The apostle attempted to proclaim the truth so Christians could detect deception. Heresy distorts truth and distracts the believer.

In Colossians, Paul describes heresy as persuasive (2:4), traditional (2:8), legalistic (2:16), mystical (2:18), and intellectual (2:23). Contrast human heresy and biblical truth.

_____

_____

_____

Heresy was prevalent during Paul's day and continues to be prevalent today. However, the truth about the person and work of Christ will always triumph over heresy. Christians can deflect heresy when you *"set your mind on what is above, not on what is on the earth"* (Colossians 3:2).

Josh McDowell is a well-known Christian speaker and writer. Years ago, as a young agnostic, Josh set out to disprove God by reading the Bible. As he read Scripture, he heard the truth, and his own human philosophy faltered. He was converted to faith in Jesus Christ as he read the Bible. Today he is recognized as a leading Christian in apologetics, the defense of the faith. Truth will always triumph over heresy and ensure intellectual well-being.

It is essential for Christians to be well *intellectually*. It is also important for us to have a good attitude about our work, to be occupationally well.

Occupational Well-Being

When God created the first people, He had a job for them—care for the creatures of the earth (Genesis 1:26–27). All humans are created for a purpose. Without a purpose or a job to do, one has little reason to live. Paul challenges believers do the work of God, to be His hands and feet in proclaiming the message of salvation. Occupational well-being results when an individual loves her work. Satisfaction in work, excellence in performance, and continued professional growth contribute to overall health and wellness.

Paul addressed the subject of occupational well-being in Colossians 1:24–29. He specifically discussed his own call to ministry and the calling of others to full-time Christian service. Paul even viewed his physical sufferings as a part of his work for the Lord. His call was from God and for the preaching of His Word (Colossians 1:25). The apostle fulfilled his call to ministry with great zeal. Whether in full-time ministry or a secular career, Christians today are called by God for a purpose. When we hear that call and understand its purpose, we should work diligently and excel professionally.

How did Paul say he worked? Read Colossians 1:29 then write the answer here.

Paul strived in his work with the help of God's strength and power. God's strength and power are available for our work too.

For 15 years, I worked as director of speech pathology in a large medical center. I was called to that work, and I loved it. Then God gave me a new call—He called me to full-time ministry as a Christian speaker, teacher, and writer. I love my new work too! Why? I love it because I am in the will of God for my life. When Christians are doing the will of God in their work, they will experience occupational wellness.

It is essential for Christians to be well *occupationally*. Another important area of wellness is physical health.

Physical Well-Being

The human body is a complex machine created perfectly by God to function smoothly. In order to function, the body must be cared for—proper physical maintenance is essential to efficient performance. For the believer, care of the body is a biblical mandate. The body is the temple of the Lord—His dwelling place (1 Corinthians 6:19). As a steward of that temple, the Christian should care for herself both spiritually and physically.

While legalistic observation of rituals is not necessary for salvation, the believer should be a good steward of what is taken into the body. Proper nutrition and regular exercise are essential to physical well-being. Adequate sleep and stress reduction also contribute to physical health.

There are several wonderful biblically based weight-control programs today like First Place and Faithfully Fit. Spiritual discipline is emphasized in concert with physical discipline. A Christian can grow spiritually while learning to control her diet. A biblical approach to weight control and regular exercise leads to physical wellness.

I always struggle with my own physical well-being. I am grateful that my mother was "The Healthiest Girl in America" so I have a family history of long life. But, I must take responsibility for maintaining my good health. A balanced diet and regular exercise are difficult due to the delicious food in New Orleans and a busy schedule. However, I must constantly discipline myself physically so that I may have energy to serve the Lord.

It is essential for Christians to be well *physically*. In addition, Christians must consider their social wellness.

Social Well-Being

Social well-being includes healthy relationships and a viable support network. The family unit is the first context for development of social skills—learning to relate to people in a happy, positive way. Friends also provide nurturing relationships. For the Christian, the church family can be a source of deep friendships. Every human being has a desire to belong to a group that gives love, support, and affirmation. Social well-being cannot be developed in isolation. People must get together, form connections, and build relationships. Many strong personal relationships last a lifetime and promote overall success.

Paul reminded the church in Colossae about the new character of the believer. In Colossians 3:12–14, he stated that new belief results in new behavior. Christians should treat people differently.

Read Colossians 3:12–14 and describe how believers should relate to other people.

_____

_____

_____

_____

The believer, a new creature, actually looks different. She takes off ungodliness and puts on virtues of godliness. Love, patience, and forgiveness should characterize the life of the Christian. When you show love to others, they will love in return. Godly behavior strengthens interpersonal relationships.

I love people! When given a choice, I would always choose to be in a room full of people than to be alone. My husband is the exact opposite. He is happiest when he is alone with a book. Whether you are a social butterfly or a recluse, you must work to improve your social relationships. My husband has worked diligently to improve his social skills because of his call to ministry. Christians can have a powerful influence on other people as they demonstrate acceptance, affirmation, and affection. Those social skills come directly from God.

It is essential for Christians to be healthy *socially*. Of course, Christians must be healthy spiritually as well as balanced in other areas of life.

Spiritual Well-Being

Faith in God and a personal relationship with Jesus Christ are key ingredients to spiritual well-being. Head knowledge without heartfelt passion does not create a healthy Christian. Instead, a Christian must have a personal faith that grows daily through Bible study, prayer, witnessing, and ministry. No one else can secure a believer's spiritual health. Every Christian must grow in faith and live out that faith in her daily life. The spiritual well-being of every Christian is God's greatest desire, but spiritual vitality will not become a reality without wellness in all dimensions of life.

In Colossians 2:6–7, Paul clearly stated the prescription for spiritual well-being: *"As you have received Christ Jesus the Lord, walk in Him, rooted and built up in Him and established in the faith."*

What does that Scripture teach you about spiritual wellness?

_____

_____

_____

If you are a true believer in Christ, you will walk in Him, living a Christ-like, set apart life.

I hear Paul's challenge to live a committed life — dependent on God, not on myself or on others, and confident in His presence and His provision. It is essential for Christians to be spiritually well.

As you conclude this study of Colossians, I pray that you are healthier and stronger spiritually now than you were when you began the study. Paul did his part to promote your spiritual wellness in his writing of this powerful book. I have tried to do my part to encourage your spiritual wellness as I directed your study of God's Word and shared my personal insights. Now it's your turn to live out what you have learned about spiritual wellness. You can do it with the help of God!

Always remember that fitness, like faith, is a journey not a destination. And, God's prescriptions in His Word are the only guarantee of good health. Be assured of my prayers for you as you live a healthy, happy Christian life!

Prescription 12 for Spiritual Wellness

"God wanted to make known to those among the Gentiles the glorious wealth of this mystery, which is **Christ in you, the hope of glory***"*
(Colossians 1:27, emphasis added).

Personal Spiritual Wellness

At this time, evaluate your overall health and wellness. How fit are you? Regardless of the answer, every Christian should strive for greater well-being.

Set at least one personal goal for wellness in each area listed below.

Emotional well-being— _____

Intellectual well-being— _____

Occupational well-being— _____

Physical well-being— _____

Social well-being— _____

Spiritual well-being— _____

Now make the commitment to accomplish these goals with the help of the Lord.

12 Prescriptions for Spiritual Wellness

1. *"Grace to you and peace from God our Father"* (Colossians 1:2).

2. *"Walk worthy of the Lord, fully pleasing [to Him], bearing fruit in every good work and growing in the knowledge of God"* (Colossians 1:10).

3. *"He is the image of the invisible God, the firstborn over all creation"* (Colossians 1:15).

4. *"I labor for this, striving with His strength that works in me"* (Colossians 1:29).

5. *"Therefore as you have received Christ Jesus the Lord, walk in Him"* (Colossians 2:6).

6. *"If you died with Christ to the elemental forces of this world, why do you live as if you still belonged to the world? Why do you submit to regulations?"* (Colossians 2:20).

7. *"Set your mind on what is above, not on what is on the earth"* (Colossians 3:2).

8. *"Above all, [put on] love — the perfect bond of unity"* (Colossians 3:14).

9. *"Whatever you do, do it enthusiastically, as something done for the Lord and not for men"* (Colossians 3:23).

10. *"Your speech should always be gracious, seasoned with salt, so that you may know how you should answer each person"* (Colossians 4:6).

11. *"'Pay attention to the ministry you have received in the Lord, so that you can accomplish it'"* (Colossians 4:17).

12. *"God wanted to make known to those among the Gentiles the glorious wealth of this mystery, which is Christ in you, the hope of glory"* (Colossians 1:27).

Group Teaching Guide

This section includes teaching suggestions for the small group leader. It also provides a format for the discussion time and a typical schedule for a one-hour session. A focus group has tried this particular approach, and it was effective. Let the Holy Spirit lead your group discussion and make any appropriate changes. These are simply teaching helps.

Lesson One: Called by Christ (Introduction)

Prayertime (5 minutes)

Ask each member of the group to write a prayer of commitment in the front of her Bible study book. Spend a few minutes in personal prayer, asking God to bless this Bible study.

Review (5 minutes)

Discuss the format for this study and details about the group meeting. Encourage each member to complete her own study before discussing it with the group.

Scripture Reading (5 minutes)

Read Colossians 1:1–2 aloud. Suggest that members circle the name of the author of this book and underline any description of him.

Group Discussion (40 minutes)

1. Discuss the medical field's focus on wellness and the Christian's need for spiritual wellness.

2. Talk about the author of Colossians. Ask:

Who wrote the Book of Colossians? (Paul)

Who was with him? (Timothy)

What do you know about Paul's birth, rebirth, life, journeys, writings, and death? (born a Jew, saved by Christ, committed life, many missionary journeys, wrote 13 New Testament epistles, died a martyr)

3. Briefly discuss the audience receiving this letter from Paul.

- the city (Colossae)

- the church (Gentile believers in Colossae)

- the conflict (dangerous false teachings)

Refer to a map of Paul's missionary journeys.

4. Discuss Paul's admonition to the church of Colossae—his warning. (Beware of heresy—false teachings.)

5. Review Paul's answers—the three central themes of the Book of Colossians.
(Christ is Creator of everything and Savior of all; the world is sinful and seeking to devour all; and Christians are vehicles of service and examples of faith)

Closing (5 minutes)

1. Read Prescription 1 for Spiritual Wellness (Colossians 1:26) aloud as a group.

2. Share personal insights about who you are in Christ.

Lesson Two: Prayer Pleases God
(Colossians 1:1–12)

Prayertime (5 minutes)

Give out index cards to each member and ask her to record one specific prayer request. Collect the cards, then distribute one card to each person. Pray silently for that particular need.

Review (5 minutes)

Review lesson 1 by asking:

Who wrote Colossians?

Why was it written?

Where was it written?

What are its themes?

To whom was it written?

Scripture Reading (5 minutes)

Ask a volunteer to read Colossians 1:1–12 aloud. Encourage all members to underline any instructions about prayer in this passage of Scripture.

Group Discussion (40 minutes)

1. Ask: *Why do you think prayer pleases God?*

2. Introduce this lesson by stating Paul's three specific ways to pray: lift up others, thank the Father, and ask for power.

3. Discuss Paul's guidelines for praying for others from Colossians 1:1–12. (see vv. 3, 9, 10, 11, and 12.)

4. Compare and contrast prayers of petition and intercession. (petition — specific requests to God for self; intercession=prayer for others)

5. Encourage members to share praises to God and thanksgiving for His blessings.

6. Ask: *Why is it important for Christians to ask God for power?*

Closing (5 minutes)

1. Go around the room and have each member read aloud one word of Prescription 2 for Spiritual Wellness (Colossians 1:10). Then read the entire passage aloud.

2. Quietly reread your prayer of commitment recorded in Personal Spiritual Wellness.

3. Share the closing salutation of Colossians with someone in the group: *"Grace to you and peace from God our Father and the Lord Jesus Christ."*

Lesson Three: The Incomparable Christ (Colossians 1:13–23)

Prayertime (5 minutes)

Read "A Hymn of Him" from Colossians 1:15–20 as a prayer. The leader should read the verses and the entire group read the chorus.

Review (5 minutes)

Review lesson 2 by asking: *What did Paul teach us about prayer?* Then ask: *What have you personally learned about prayer this week?*

Scripture Reading (5 minutes)

Ask one member of the group to read the entire focal passage aloud: Colossians 1:13–23.

Group Discussion (40 minutes)

1. Define *Christology* and briefly discuss its importance to the Christian. (the study of Christ's nature and person)

2. Ask participants to name some of the descriptors of Christ found in Colossians 1:13–23. (deliverer, redeemer, forgiver, God, firstborn, creator, ruler, eternal, head of church, reconciler)

3. Discuss the fact that Christ is fully God and fully man. Refer to several Scripture references in this lesson.

4. Rejoice together as you share specific creations of God.

5. Ask: *What does the Bible teach about Christ as Head of the church?*

6. Discuss *reconciliation* and how Christ reconciles the world. (renewal of friendship; harmonizing of apparently opposed ideas)

Closing (5 minutes)

1. Read Prescription 3 for Spiritual Wellness (Colossians 1:15) aloud as a group, slowly and deliberately.

2. Ask members to relate how Christ makes Himself known to them on a daily basis.

Lesson Four: Rejoice in Suffering (Colossians 1:24–29)

Prayertime (5 minutes)

Follow this model for prayer as you voice sentence prayers to the Father.

A—adoration

C—confession

T—thanksgiving

S—supplication

Review (5 minutes)

Review the teachings about Christ found in lesson 3 as you ask these questions:

Who is Christ?

What did He create?

What is His relationship to the church?

How does He reconcile us to the Father?

Why is Christ incomparable?

Scripture Reading (5 minutes)

If you have access to *The Message*, read Colossians 1:24–29 in that modern paraphrase. Paul's perspective on suffering is very clear in this passage.

Group Discussion (40 minutes)

1. Briefly discuss three challenges Christians experience: human suffering, the mysteries of the faith, and the call to service.

2. Ask: *Do you believe that suffering is experienced by Christians today?* Review Paul's five reasons to rejoice in suffering. (closer relationship to Christ, assures salvation, future reward, temporary, privilege)

3. Discuss the mystery of the faith. Ask: *Are there specific things that you don't understand about God? What?*

4. Ask several members of the group to share their calls to ministry.

5. Conclude the discussion by asking: *Why should Christians work so hard for the gospel?* (Colossians 1:28)

Closing (5 minutes)

1. Read Prescription 4 for Spiritual Wellness (Colossians 1:29) aloud, then ask several members to restate the verse.

2. Have members pray about their own commitments to proclaiming the gospel.

Lesson Five: Built Up in Christ (Colossians 2:1–15)

Prayertime (5 minutes)

Ask members to pray in groups of three. Pray specifically for each person to be "built up in Christ."

Review (5 minutes)

Review the summary points of lesson 4—human suffering, the mysteries of the faith, and the call to service. Did anyone complete her gospel "to-do" list this week? Ask members to share what they learned.

Scripture Reading (5 minutes)

Ask five people to read the focal Scripture by section:

1. Colossians 2:1–3;

2. Colossians 2:4–5;

3. Colossians 2:6–7;

4. Colossians 2:8–10; and

5. Colossians 2:11–15.

Group Discussion (40 minutes)

1. Begin the discussion by asking, *What does it mean to be built up in Christ?*

2. Discuss how Christians should run the race. Read Philippians 3:12–14.

3. List the six verbs from Colossians 2:1–7 on the board—*know, encourage, knit, say, receive, walk*. Discuss what these verbs teach about being "rooted in Christ."

4. Ask members to paraphrase Colossians 2:8, Paul's warning to believers.

5. Briefly discuss the ordinance of baptism, including ways to celebrate with new converts.

6. Challenge the group to practice biblical forgiveness as taught by Paul in Colossians 2:13–14.

Closing (5 minutes)

1. Read Prescription 5 for Spiritual Wellness (Colossians 2:6), then ask members to suggest verbs to replace *walk* (example: so *live* in Him, so *talk* in Him, etc.).

2. How spiritually strong is your group? Ask each member to write her total spiritual weight from the Spiritual Wellness activity on a piece of paper that is passed around. Add up the score and announce it. Then pray that God will strengthen the members individually and collectively as a group.

Lesson Six: Spiritual Nutrition
(Colossians 2:16–23)

Prayertime (5 minutes)

Spend time praying these Scriptures from the Book of Colossians. Read each verse aloud then allow time for silent prayer: Colossians 1:2b; 1:9; 1:12; 2:6–7; 4:17–18; 1:3; 1:10–11; 1:24; 4:2.

Review (5 minutes)

Draw a tree on the board as you review lesson 5. Ask this question: *How can you be rooted in Him?*

Scripture Reading (5 minutes)

Ask each person to read silently Colossians 2:16–23 as you begin your discussion of this passage.

Group Discussion (40 minutes)

1. Ask how group members practice spiritual nutrition.

2. Turn in your Bibles to Leviticus 11–15 and skim these chapters in order to mention some of the Jewish regulations. Note how many very specific rules they had to follow.

3. Discuss what the people in Colossae added to faith (asceticism, observances, visions, angels).

4. Compare and contrast what is meant by a *guru* and a *mentor*. How have mentors positively influenced your lives? (guru=a human leader who seeks personal attention; mentor=a Christ-like individual who focuses attention on God)

5. Review these false teachings: half-truths, false humility, sinful pride, and unnecessary slavery.

6. Ask members to explain the difference between salvation by faith and salvation by works.

Closing (5 minutes)

1. Ask one member of the group to read Prescription 6 for Spiritual Wellness (Colossians 2:20).

2. In conclusion, have another person read Galatians 2:18–21 for comparison.

Lesson Seven: Healthy Christian Living (Colossians 3:1–11)

Prayertime (5 minutes)

Write the following topics on index cards and give to six members of the group: *Praise to God, Members of Bible Study Group, The Church,*

Christian Friends, Unsaved Friends, Thanksgiving to God. Ask each one to voice a topical sentence prayer.

Review (5 minutes)

Review lesson 6 briefly by asking:

What are additives to faith?

What is the diet guru?

Scripture Reading (5 minutes)

Divide the group into three smaller groups. Ask each small group to read and briefly discuss one of the following Scripture passages: Colossians 3:1–4; Colossians 3:5–7; and Colossians 3:8–14.

Group Discussion (40 minutes)

1. Discuss the dangers of legalism of the law (Colossians 2:20) and forgiveness of God (Colossians 3:2).

2. Ask the group to share some things they worry about, then read Philippians 4:6.

3. Review these three helpful hints about healthy Christian living: be consistent, be real, be godly.

4. Summarize what several New Testament Scriptures teach about the wrath of God. (See John 3:36; Romans 1:18; Romans 2:5; 1 Thessalonians 1:10.)

5. List on the board what behaviors Christians are to "put off" (Colossians 3:8–9) and "put on" (Colossians 3:12–14). (Put off—anger, wrath, malice, slander, filthy language, lying; Put on—compassion, kindness, humility, gentleness, patience, acceptance, forgiveness, love)

6. Conclude the discussion by completing the Scripture statements about healthy Christian living.

Closing (5 minutes)

1. Ask each member to silently study Prescription 7 for Spiritual Wellness (Colossians 3:2), and then recite it from memory as a group.

2. Review the six previous Prescriptions for Spiritual Wellness.

Lesson Eight: Dress for Success (Colossians 3:12–17)

Prayertime (5 minutes)

Ask each person to find a prayer partner and spend time praying in this manner: praise to God, petition for others, prayer for self.

Review (5 minutes)

Review lesson 7 before you begin this study. Pose this question: *Why is it important for Christians to be consistent, to be real, and to be godly?*

Scripture Reading (5 minutes)

Ask a volunteer in the group to read Colossians 3:12–17 aloud.

Group Discussion (40 minutes)

1. As a group, brainstorm items of clothing they would want to take on a trip. Write the clothing on the board. Use the process of elimination to decide on only eight items.

2. Review the suggested eight-piece wardrobe in this lesson. (jacket, dress, pants, shirt, skirt, scarf, shoes, purse)

3. Discuss the Christian's spiritual wardrobe: kindness, humility, gentleness, patience, acceptance, forgiveness, and love.

4. Ask why love is the essential virtue of Christian living.

5. Read Ephesians 6:13–18, then discuss the Christian's wardrobe for spiritual warfare. (belt of truth, breastplate of righteousness, shoes of the gospel, shield of faith, helmet of salvation, word of Spirit)

6. Complete your discussion by asking: *How do you personally resist spiritual warfare?*

Closing (5 minutes)

1. Call on members of the group to read Prescription 8 for Spiritual Wellness (Colossians 3:14) in as many different translations of the Bible as represented among the group.

2. Ask individuals to call out specific behaviors that Christians should "take off" and "put on" that they recorded for this week's Personal Spiritual Wellness.

Lesson Nine: A Submissive Heart (Colossians 3:18–4:1)

Prayertime (5 minutes)

Begin this group session with a directed quiet time. Ask members to pray silently following this model written on the board:

Praise to God

Confession of Sin

Requests for Self (physical needs, mental needs, spiritual needs)

Confidence in God

Review (5 minutes)

Review lesson 8—the believer's personal wardrobe and spiritual wardrobe. Ask members if they cleaned their spiritual wardrobes this week. What behaviors did they alter?

Scripture Reading (5 minutes)

Have three members of the group read a section of the Scripture focus aloud: Colossians 3:18–19; Colossians 3:20–21; and Colossians 3:22 to 4:1.

Group Discussion (40 minutes)

1. Pose this question as you begin today's lesson: *Who has authority in your life?*

2. Ask members to share their definitions of biblical submission. (willingly giving control of your life to someone in authority over you because of your love for the Lord)

3. Fill in the blanks together to complete God's design for human relationships (Colossians 3:18–4:1). (husbands, wives, parents, children, masters, servants)

4. Discuss how wives submit to their husbands (see Ephesians 5:33). (notice, honor, prefer, esteem, defer to, praise, regard, love, admire)

5. Discuss how children submit to parents. (continue always to obey parents)

6. Discuss how employees submit to employers. (willingly follow their employees)

Closing (5 minutes)

1. Read Prescription 9 for Spiritual Wellness (Colossians 3:23) aloud, then discuss why it is important to do everything "heartily."

2. Encourage each member to draw a heart in the Bible study book and write this prayer of commitment in it: *Lord, I submit my heart to You and to all people in authority over me.*

Lesson Ten: The Speech of a Believer (Colossians 4:2–6)

Prayertime (5 minutes)

As members come in, ask them to turn in their Bibles to Psalm 23 and spend time meditating on this prayer of David.

Review (5 minutes)

Review Paul's teaching about submission in human relationships from lesson 9: wives to husbands, children to parents, employees to employers.

Scripture Reading (5 minutes)

Ask members to underline in their Bibles the words *pray, speak,* and *walk* as you read aloud Colossians 4:2–6.

Group Discussion (40 minutes)

1. Reflect on Paul's teachings about behavior.

2. Discuss why Paul was so concerned about the behavior of Christians.

3. Ask: *What does Paul teach about prayer in Colossians 4:2–6?*

4. Ask: *Why must Christians speak of Him?*

5. Ask: *How do Christians speak of Him in actions?*

6. Discuss the difference between worldly wisdom and spiritual wisdom. (See 1 Corinthians 3:18–4:5.)

Closing (5 minutes)

1. Write Prescription 10 for Spiritual Wellness (Colossians 4:6) on the board substituting *my/ your* and *I/ you* (two times). Read it aloud together.

2. Ask members to suggest words of kindness that can "season their speech with salt."

Lesson Eleven: A Fond Farewell
(Colossians 4:7–18)

Prayertime (5 minutes)

For today's prayertime, repeat The Lord's Prayer (Matthew 6:9–13) aloud together, slowly and prayerfully.

Review (5 minutes)

Review lesson 10, "The Speech of a Believer." Discuss how Christians should speak to God, speak of Him, and speak like Him.

Scripture Reading (5 minutes)

Ask the group to read Colossians 4:7–18 silently and circle the names of all co-workers in ministry mentioned by Paul.

Group Discussion (40 minutes)

1. Briefly describe the format of typical Greco-Roman correspondence. (personal introductions, greetings, final blessing)

2. Ask the group to help you list on the board the ten co-workers identified by Paul in Colossians 4:7–18. Practice pronouncing their names correctly. (Tychicus, Onesimus, Aristarchus, Mark, Justus, Epaphras, Luke, Demas, Nympha, Archippus)

3. Discuss each individual identified by Paul in his introductions.

4. Underline the names of those individuals listed on the board who actually ministered with Paul. (Aristarchus, Epaphras, Luke, Demas)

5. Suggest definitions of an *epistle*. (a biblical letter of instruction)

6. Consider why Paul concludes his letters with *grace*.

Closing (5 minutes)

1. Ask members to meditate for a few minutes on Prescription 11 for Spiritual Wellness (Colossians 4:17).

2. Conclude today's study by reading aloud Paul's closing exhortations and blessing in Colossians 4:16–18.

Lesson Twelve: Faith and Fitness (Conclusion)

Prayertime (5 minutes)

Today's opening prayer will be for unbelievers. Ask each person to write down the name of one unsaved friend, and then spend time praying for that person's spiritual wellness.

Review (5 minutes)

Review the names of the ten individuals mentioned by Paul in lesson 11 (Colossians 4:7–18). Briefly describe who they were.

Scripture Reading (5 minutes)

Ask six volunteers to read these selected Scriptures from the Book of Colossians: Colossians 1:24–29; Colossians 2:1–3; Colossians 2:6–7; Colossians 2:8–10; Colossians 2:16–23; and Colossians 3:12–14.

Group Discussion (40 minutes)

1. Reflect on the teachings in Colossians that should influence a believer's daily life. (See lesson 12.)

2. Ask someone to read 1 Thessalonians 5:23 from the New American Standard Bible, and then discuss what Paul meant by *wellness*.

3. Draw a circle on the board and divide it into six equal parts, and then label each section as follows: *emotional, intellectual, occupational, physical, social, spiritual*.

4. Discuss each aspect of a Christian's well-being.

5. Share practical ways for Christians to maintain wellness in each area.

Closing (5 minutes)

1. Read aloud together Prescription 12 for Spiritual Wellness (Colossians 1:27), a theme verse in the Book of Colossians.

2. Ask members to share the Prescription for Spiritual Wellness that has meant the most to them personally.

Bibliography

Baker, Robert H. *A Basic Guide to Interpreting the Bible.* Grand Rapids, MI: Baker, 1994.

Barclay, William. *The Letters to the Philippians, Colossians, and Thessalonians.* Philadelphia: The Westminster Press, 1975.

Burroughs, Esther. *A Garden Path to Mentoring.* Birmingham: New Hope, 1997.

Butler, Trent C., gen. ed. *Holman Bible Dictionary.* Nashville: Holman Bible Publishers, 1991.

Cooper, Kenneth H. *It's Better to Believe: The New Medical Program that Uses Spiritual Motivation to Achieve Maximum Health and Add Years to Your Life.* Nashville: Thomas Nelson, 1995.

Dunnam, Maxie D. *The Communicator's Commentary: Galatians, Ephesians, Philippians, Colossians, Philemon.* Waco: Word Books, 1982.

"God the Son." *Baptist Faith and Message.* 2000. The Southern Baptist Convention. December 7, 2009, http://sbc.net/bfm/bfm2000.asp.

Hendriksen, William. *New Testament Commentary: Colossians and Philemon.* Grand Rapids: Baker Book House, 1964.

MacArthur, John, Jr. *The MacArthur New Testament Commentary: Colossians and Philemon.* Chicago: Moody Press, 1992.

McGinn, Linda. *Equipped for Life: Ephesians, Philippians, Colossians.* Grand Rapids: Baker Books, 1994.

Mullins, E. Y. *Studies in Colossians.* Nashville: Sunday School Board of the Southern Baptist Convention, 1935.

Nelson's Complete Book of Bible Maps and Charts. Nashville: Thomas Nelson Publishers, 1993.

Patterson, Dorothy Kelley and Rhonda Harrington Kelley (eds.). *The Woman's Study Bible.* Nashville: Thomas Nelson, 1995.

— — —. *Women's Evangelical Commentary: New Testament.* Nashville: Holman Reference, 2006.

Severance, W. Murray. *Pronouncing Bible Names.* Nashville: Holman Bible Publishers, 1985.

Simpson, E. K. and F. F. Bruce. *The New International Commentary on the New Testament: Commentary on the Epistles to the Ephesians and Colossians.* Grand Rapids: William B. Eerdmans Publishing, 1973.

Smith, Hannah Whitall. *The Christian's Secret to a Happy Life.* Westwood, NJ: Barbour and Company, 1985.

Smith, Pamela M. *Food for Life.* Lake Mary, FL: Creation House, 1994.

The Woman's Study Bible. Nashville: Thomas Nelson, 1995.

Wright, N. T. *Tyndale New Testament Commentaries: Colossians and Philemon.* Grand Rapids: William B. Eerdmans Publishing Co., 1978.

Yessick, Tommy. *Building Blocks for Longer Life and Ministry.* Nashville: LifeWay Christian Resources, 1997.

Journal

Journal

Journal

Journal

Other Books in
"A Woman's Guide" Series

True Contentment
A Biblical Study for Achieving Satisfaction in Life
Rhonda Harrington Kelley
ISBN-10: 1-59669-260-X
ISBN-13: 978-1-59669-260-2

Personal Holiness
A Biblical Study for Developing a Holy Lifestyle
Rhonda Harrington Kelley
ISBN-10: 1-59669-257-X
ISBN-13: 978-1-59669-257-2

Available in bookstores
everywhere.

For information about these books or any New Hope product,
visit www.newhopepublishers.com.